SECRET
MONTEREY

A Guide to the Weird, Wonderful, and Obscure

David Laws

Reedy Press
PO Box 5131
St. Louis, MO 63139
www.reedypress.com

Library of Congress Control Number: 2021948916
ISBN: 9781681063652

Design by Jill Halpin

Unless otherwise indicated, all photos are courtesy of the author
or in the public domain.

We (the publisher and the author) have done our best to provide the most
accurate information available when this book was completed. However, we
make no warranty, guarantee, or promise about the accuracy, completeness, or
currency of the information provided, and we expressly disclaim all warranties,
express or implied. Please note that attractions, company names, addresses,
websites, and phone numbers are subject to change or closure, and this is
outside of our control. We are not responsible for any loss, damage, injury, or
inconvenience that may occur due to the use of this book. When exploring new
destinations, please do your homework before you go. You are responsible for
your own safety and health when using this book.

Printed in the United States of America
22 23 24 25 26   5 4 3 2 1

This book is dedicated to my late wife, Jean,
who shared many of the adventures that informed the stories
in this book. And to my boys, Mark and Matt, who are always kind
in their comments about their dad's words and pictures.

CONTENTS

v

ACKNOWLEDGMENTS

A huge thank-you to everyone who contributed in any way to the publication of *Secret Monterey*. Many of you helped directly with specific ideas, information, and encouragement during the early days of the pandemic when colleges, libraries, museums, and other traditional resources were inaccessible.

To all students of Ken Ottmar's Winter 2021 Creative Writing class at the Pacific Grove Adult Education Center and particularly to Ann Folsom, Clare Manning, Diane Gsell, Evelyn Kahan, Joanna Daum, Steve Wheeler, Terry Coen, and, of course, Ken, for their detailed reviews of the content.

Others contributed by introducing me to the secrets and wonders of Monterey County, especially Michele Crompton (OLLI at CSUMB), David Gubernick (photographing the back roads), Tom Rolander (Digital Research and the Gary Kildall story), Susan Shillinglaw (Steinbeck Country), and Steven Hauk of Hauk Fine Arts (artists and photographers of the county).

And to all members of the Rotary Club of Pacific Grove, who welcomed me to the community and were generous with their comments whenever I gave talks on topics covered in the book. I am donating all profits from the first printing of *Secret Monterey* to the Club's Legacy Fund that provides funds to organizations serving the citizens of our community and beyond.

INTRODUCTION

Monterey is the third-largest agricultural county in the third-largest state of the Union and plays a vital role in producing fine food and wine for tables across the nation. And having recovered from near extinction, the Monterey Bay fishery once again yields a bountiful harvest of seafood. Another important local economic driver, hospitality, takes advantage of this fortunate confluence of epicurean bounty to deliver cuisine at the peak of freshness and flavor. But there is more than just food and wine to be enjoyed across Monterey's diverse combination of climates, cultures, and geography that has long been described as California's greatest and most scenic playground.

From a foggy coast of mountains and cool marine waters to the verdant Salinas Valley and on to the blazing-hot inland ranges, where tectonic forces continue to shape the landscape, there are countless weird, wonderful, and obscure people, places, and stories for you to discover. Monterey's unique history as the only community in North America to have lived under the flags of four colonial powers only adds to its fund of legends, myths, and stories.

Secret Monterey includes 84 vignettes on unusual, little-known, and underappreciated aspects of the region. Some places and events, such as the Monterey Bay Aquarium, Pebble Beach Concours d'Elegance, and the Big Sur Coast, are far from secret. However, even these popular attractions have elements seldom revealed in traditional travel guides. I have explored and photographed every location described in this book, and I continue to be excited about uncovering unexpected details, people, and stories. I hope that you will enjoy the same thrill of discovery.

WHERE ZOMBIE WORMS DINE ON WHALE BONES

Where is the Monterey Canyon?

The Monterey Bay Aquarium Research Institute (MBARI) at Moss Landing is just a mile or so from one of the deepest submarine canyons off the coast of North America. Reaching over 16,000 feet below the ocean's surface, the height of the Monterey Submarine Canyon's vertical walls rival those of the Grand Canyon. The ability to penetrate these depths so close to land gives unprecedented access to study the myriad and often bizarre-looking creatures of the deep sea.

Using remotely operated submarine vehicles (ROVs), in 2004 MBARI researchers discovered a new tubeworm species. They called them "zombie worms" for their diet of dead whale bones and named the species *Osedax*, Latin for bone-devourer. First encountered a mile below the surface, *Osedax* have no eyes, mouth, or stomach. Instead, they employ roots to burrow into nutrient-rich bones scattered in whale boneyards across the ocean floor.

MBARI's ocean research vessels can sometimes be seen docked opposite the institute's offices in Moss Landing Harbor. Painted bright yellow, *ROV Doc Ricketts* is capable of diving to more than 13,000 feet. A twin-hull support vessel for the ROV, the *R/V Western Flyer*, has a center well whose floor opens to launch *Doc Ricketts* directly into the water below. Both vessel

Steinbeck based the character of "Doc" in the novel *Cannery Row* on the personality of his friend Ed Ricketts, although he never referred to him in print as "Doc Ricketts."

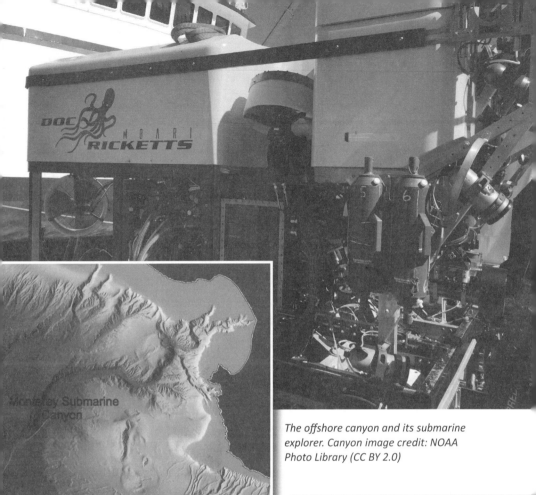

The offshore canyon and its submarine explorer. Canyon image credit: NOAA Photo Library (CC BY 2.0)

names honor philosopher and biologist Edward F. Ricketts for his pioneering work on marine ecology and his voyage on the fishing boat *Western Flyer*, as told by John Steinbeck in *The Log from the Sea of Cortez*. The original *Western Flyer* is being restored in Port Townsend, Washington. Plans are to return the vessel to Monterey for ocean-related educational programs.

DENIZENS OF THE DEEP

WHAT: Monterey Bay Aquarium Research Institute

WHERE: 7700 Sandholdt Rd., Moss Landing, CA

COST: : Free to tour on scheduled public open days

PRO TIP: The *R/V Western Flyer* will be replaced in 2022 by a new vessel to be named *R/V David Packard* after the tech titan and MBARI founder.

RAFTS OF SEA OTTERS

Where is the best place to watch sea otters?

The California sea otter's (*Enhydra lutris nereis*) expressive face, thick fur coat, and skill at carrying their pups on their chest make them one of Monterey County's most endearing creatures. Hunted to near extinction by fur traders in the 19th century, the local population has rebounded to around 3,000 otters under federal protection.

You can watch individual otters at play in sheltered coves and inlets all along the coast. To see large groups, called rafts, visit the Elkhorn Slough National Estuarine Research Reserve. Researchers have recorded counts above 100 individuals near the area where the slough waters flow into Moss Landing Harbor and out into the bay. You can see them from the shoreline, but the best viewing is from your own or a rented kayak, or from a guided nature tour boat. Both depart from Moss Landing Harbor.

Meandering seven miles inland from the coast, Elkhorn Slough comprises the largest tract of tidal salt marsh in California outside of San Francisco Bay. Carved by an ancient river, the San Andreas earthquake fault moved its course away from the coast, leaving behind a dry valley. Over the last 10,000 years, rising ocean levels filled the void to form the slough as an arm of the sea.

Educational exhibits, naturalist programs, and access to waterfront hiking trails are available at the reserve visitor center, located about six miles inland at 1700 Elkhorn Road, Watsonville.

Top: *Tour boat passengers see otters up-close.*

Inset: *Mother otter and pup. Photo courtesy of Linda Abbey, Nature Photography*

In addition to the playful otters, the slough harbors raucous sea lions, curious seals, and hundreds of resident and migratory bird species, as well as leopard and smoothhound sharks. Although their dorsal fins may look menacing, these shark species are smaller and less scary than the abundant great whites that frequent the open bay.

SEE OTTER HAVEN

WHAT: Sea otters at play

WHERE: Elkhorn Slough, near Moss Landing Harbor

COST: Free from the shore or by personal kayak

PRO TIP: Kayaks and nature tour boats are popular. Reserve ahead if possible.

TURNS STRAW INTO GOLD

Looking for that special item?

"We will turn straw into gold by seeing the beauty and potential in disregarded people and discarded things and by communicating to others a reverence for all that is in our care." These lines are from an inspirational speech at the recent reopening of the Last Chance Mercantile, a thrift store at the Monterey Regional Waste Management District (MRWMD) facility, better known to locals as "The Dump."

MRWMD started The Last Chance Mercantile in 1991 as a monthly flea market and auction. In 1996 it moved to the current large building with a paved, two-acre yard in Marina. The mercantile recycles and sells at affordable prices everything from construction and landscape materials to reusable household items of every imaginable variety that are donated or picked up by the county's garbage collection contractors. Managed by the Veterans Transition Center of California, the operation provides employment

YOU'LL FIND IT HERE

WHAT: Last Chance Mercantile thrift store

WHERE: 14201 Del Monte Blvd., Marina, CA

COST: Free

PRO TIP: If you can't find it inside, be sure to check the yard outside.

MRWMD's Small Planet School Education Garden, adjacent to the mercantile, teaches students how to reduce waste by reuse in a garden environment.

The Mercantile offers one-of-a-kind items ranging from books to boats, scrap lumber to furniture, and clothing to household treasures.

opportunities for veterans to move from crisis to self-sufficiency. It's a magical place where trash is turned into treasure. Every visit is an adventure.

The Visual and Public Art (VPA) Program at California State University, Monterey Bay and MRWMD have teamed up to create an Artist in Residence Program. This allows VPA students to salvage discarded materials and upcycle them into art. The artists work and create in the yard at the Last Chance Mercantile so the public can watch and engage with the process.

PURPLE PIPES PRODUCE PRODUCTIVE PASTURES

Why are those pipes painted purple?

Bright-purple-colored irrigation pipes and valves stand out in agricultural fields close to the ocean. Monterey County farmers grow more than 50 percent of the nation's artichokes, broccoli, celery, and lettuce, as well as large percentages of the strawberries and other produce. A combination of cool summer climate, rich alluvial soil, and abundant irrigation water makes the land bordering California Highway One south of Moss Landing, once known as Cauliflower Boulevard, particularly productive.

Generations of over-pumping groundwater for irrigation depleted aquifers close to the bay. Invading seawater turned once-pristine wells into saline reservoirs. Even supposedly salt-tolerant varieties of artichokes failed as salinity increased. Technology improvements in the

Water reclaimed specifically for use on crops is preferred by growers, as it remains high in nitrogen, phosphorus, potassium, and micronutrients that enhance yields, compared to regular groundwater.

Recycled water is important for the local strawberry crop.

treatment of sewage water in 1998 made effluent from Monterey Peninsula communities safe to use on crops. Approved only for non-potable uses, the pipes and valves that deliver recycled water are painted a distinctive shade of purple to prevent accidental misuse for drinking purposes.

Recent advancements in purification technology produce water that meets California's safe drinking standards so it can be used for human consumption. Used water is sent to the Monterey One Water regional treatment plant in Marina, where it is cleaned by processing though numerous steps that include adding ozone, microfiltration, reverse osmosis, and exposure to ultraviolet light. The plant injects this potable water into wells, where it is stored and later pumped back into the public supply.

WHERE MARILYN REIGNED AS ARTICHOKE QUEEN

Is an artichoke a fruit or a vegetable?

The globe or green artichoke (*Cynara cardunculus var. scolymus*) is the official state vegetable of California. Although it is a member of the thistle family, you can eat the fleshy base and outer leaves of the bud that is harvested before it flowers. So, like broccoli that we eat before their yellow blooms appear, artichokes are vegetables.

As vegetables go, the artichoke is among the most visually fascinating. The plant grows to a width of about six feet and three to four feet high. If the choke is not harvested from the plant, its bud eventually blossoms into a beautiful but inedible blue-violet thistle flower. Italian immigrants brought them to California in the late 19th century. Castroville farmer Andrew Molera kickstarted commercial production when he planted an acre of artichokes on his ranch in the 1920s.

On a promotional junket for a Salinas jewelry store, 22-year-old Marilyn Monroe (who was still known as Norma Jean Baker) came to town in 1948. Enthralled with the aspiring starlet, entrepreneurial artichoke growers presented her with a sash proclaiming her "California Artichoke Queen."

GIANT ARTICHOKE

WHAT: Large concrete artichoke

WHERE: The Giant Artichoke, 11261 Merritt St., Castroville, CA

COST: Free to look

PRO TIP: The Giant Artichoke's most popular menu items are deep-fried artichoke hearts.

Left: *The Giant Artichoke Restaurant*

Right: *Marilyn as "Artichoke Queen"*

In 1963, Ray Bei built the World's Largest Artichoke, a 20-foot-high, bright-green concrete replica, outside his Giant Artichoke restaurant and vegetable stand on the main thoroughfare. As nearly two-thirds of the world's artichokes are grown in the fields around Castroville, the town claims the title of "The Artichoke Center of the World."

The annual Artichoke Festival, held at the Monterey County Fairgrounds, celebrates all things artichoke with food, parades, music, art, field tours, and a promise that "Thistle Be Fun."

GRAFFITI PORTAL TO THE PARK

Is it art or vandalism?

The county's biggest art galleries are the walls of commercial buildings, barns, and other vertical outdoor surfaces. Hundreds of murals illustrate every aspect of local culture and history. But not all are appreciated as art. Tagged with street graffiti, the vandalized military housing awaiting demolition behind broken wire fences on the former Fort Ord presents gritty scenes of desolation and destruction. The Divarty Street underpass of Highway One in Marina leads from this apocalyptic setting to Fort Ord Dunes State Park's pristine coastal landscape. Visitors using this pedestrian entrance must pass through an extraordinary portal of colorful graffiti commentary on social and political issues.

Years of spray-painted images, logos, and text layer the tunnel's concrete walls to create the county's longest and most dynamic mural. It's dynamic in the sense that themes change overnight as new taggers over-tag the over-tagging of earlier "artists." Political slogans, obscenities, fantastical creatures, gang symbols, and just plain mayhem merge into a riotous mélange of colorful, abstract expression. Some see this as art. Others decry the desecration of public property.

Opened in 1917, Fort Ord served as the US Army's primary facility for basic training until being decommissioned

GRAFFITI ART

WHAT: Graffiti-lined tunnel

WHERE: Divarty Street at First Avenue, Marina, CA

COST: Free

PRO TIP: Parking at the Divarty Street tunnel entrance is not secure. Visitors to the state park should use the 8th Street entrance.

Left: *Layers of graffiti cover the walls of Divarty Street underpass in Marina.*

Inset: *Mural artists Kaitlin Ziesmer and John Van Horden at work in Sand City's West End.*

in 1991. Before taggers added their contributions, the complex exhibited a wide variety of mural renderings, from military crests and scenic views to "soldier art" scrawled across barracks walls. Typical examples are preserved in the Fort Ord Digital Collection on the Digital Commons website of California State University, Monterey Bay (digitalcommons.csumb.edu/fortord).

To discourage tagging while building a public art collection, the tiny industrial community of Sand City (pop. 405) sponsors programs that have produced three dozen or more colorful murals.

13

MILITARY MEMENTOES

Why can't I visit the Impossible City?

Named for Civil War veteran General Edward Ord, Fort Ord served as a US Army infantry training base from 1917 to 1991. Here one and a half million American soldiers enjoyed their first taste of military discipline. Much of the former administrative area is home to the California State University, Monterey Bay (CSUMB) campus. The remainder of the complex, an inland tract half the size of San Francisco, is managed by the Bureau of Land Management as Fort Ord National Monument. Nearly 15,000 acres of public open space contain 96 numbered trails. Popular recreational activities range from bird-watching and wildflower hikes to mountain biking and cross-country running.

In addition to rare plants and birds, watchtowers, trail names such as Machine Gun Flats, and other mementoes from the years of military occupation are scattered across the landscape. Two are related to its time of cavalry service. An 80-foot-long concrete watering trough built for horses of the 11th

COMANCHE'S GRAVE

WHAT: Grave of cavalry horse

WHERE: Trail #14, Ft. Ord National Monument

COST: Free

PRO TIP: Red trail markers indicate a closed trail. For your safety, never use a closed trail.

Eleven miles of the 1,200-mile De Anza National Historic Trail, from Nogales, Arizona to San Francisco, cut through the eastern corner of the monument.

Top: *Comache's grave*

Inset: *The cavalry horse watering trough*

"Blackhorse" Cavalry Regiment and the 76th Field Artillery before WWII stands alongside trail #14. A few yards away, a weathered split-stake fence encloses the grave of Comanche, one of the last cavalry horses to serve Fort Ord. Sergeant Allan MacDonald, who trained and rode Comanche for 23 years, received permission to bury her on this spot. Deep in the heart of the monument, the bizarre "Impossible City" of more than 20 cinderblock buildings designed for urban warfare exercises remains off-limits to civilians behind high gates and coils of razor wire, as it continues to be used for police and Naval Postgraduate School training activities.

Explosive munition hazards, mementoes you do not wish to encounter, still are being cleared from the southwest section of the monument. The area is closed to the public until the work is complete.

A TALE OF TWO CROSSES

Why are they controversial?

Captain Don Gaspar de Portola led an overland expedition to locate Monterey Bay, as described by mariner Sebastián Vizcaino in 1602. As Portola failed to recognize the site, his party continued north, and they stumbled across San Francisco Bay on October 28, 1769. Not a bad consolation prize. On their return journey, they erected two large wooden crosses overlooking the coast near Monterey as signals to their supply ship that, unknown to them, had been lost at sea.

A bronze plaque titled Portola-Crespi Monument, mounted on Del Monte Beach immediately south of the Monterey Tides Hotel, reads: "In the winter of 1769, the Spanish expedition in search of Monterey Bay, under the command of Portola and Father Juan Crespi, erected a cross on or near this site and left the following message: 'The land expedition is returning to San Diego for lack of provisions today, December 9, 1769.'" The second cross stood on Carmel Meadows, overlooking Carmel River State Beach.

Harry Downie, who led the restoration of Mission Carmel, built two 20-foot-high redwood replicas to replace the original crosses that had long disappeared. Erected in 1944, the Carmel replica fell in a storm in 1983, but local volunteers quickly replaced it. To mark the 100th anniversary of Portola's expedition, the Monterey replica was installed on Del Monte

Portola's 1769 expedition did not recognize Monterey from Vizcaino's description, due to heavy fog. See the vignette on "June Gloom" (p. 154). Portola was successful in his second attempt in 1770.

Left: *Del Monte Beach cross site is marked with a plaque.*

Inset: *Carmel Meadows cross replica*

CROSSED SIGNALS

WHAT: Crosses on public land stir controversy

WHERE: Del Monte Beach, Monterey and Carmel Meadows, CA

COST: Free

PRO TIP: Calle La Cruz, near the Carmel cross, has limited parking. A more scenic approach is a one-mile, bluff-top walk from Carmel Meadows trailhead.

Beach in 1969. After vandals sawed this second cross down in 2009, attempts to replace it unleashed a constitutional crisis. As the American Civil Liberties Union (ACLU) threatened to sue the city for placing a religious symbol on public property, the repaired cross now stands in San Carlos Catholic Cemetery. Bishop of Monterey Daniel Garcia noted that, as it overlooks Dennis the Menace Park, perhaps it will "help Dennis to not be so mischievous."

WORLD'S WORST CAR SHOW

What does it take to win?

An irreverent and sardonic attitude toward the exclusivity and extravagance of the Pebble Beach Concours d'Elegance sets the Concours d'LeMons apart from the 40-plus other annual events of Monterey Car Week (a.k.a. Classic Car Week or Monterey Auto Week). As described on the organizers' website, the show is "an ugly oil stain on auto week. Hoopties, Rust Buckets, Misfits, Mistakes, and the worst of the automotive world are on display, and as always, celebrity judges will accept bribes for our thrift shop-sourced trophies."

This counterculture concours is held at Seaside City Hall on the same weekend in August as the flagship Pebble Beach event. Featuring only the finest in oddball, mundane, and truly awful offerings from the automotive world, the Concours d'LeMons honors aesthetic and technological underachievement. The organizers advise: "Get a tetanus shot, bring your sense of humor and embrace the wacky folks who love it."

The "idiot behind the whole thing," Head Gasket Alan Galbraith, recalls that "according to court records and arrest warrants," the first event took place in 2009. Judges rank winning vehicles in categories such as "Worst of Show" and

---

Similar counterculture concours events are held in Florida, Michigan, Missouri, Washington, and Canada (at a really cool place where the moose don't bother us).

They brought their sense of humor to the "ugly stain on Auto Week."

COUNTERCULTURE CONCOURS

WHAT: Concours d'LeMons

WHERE: Seaside City Hall, 440 Harcourt Ave., Seaside, CA

COST: Free

PRO TIP: Busy, street parking only, so get there early

"Rustbelt American Junk" for their peeling paint, rust content, and sheer absurdity. A rejection letter from a major d'Elegance event scores extra points, and the car with the highest emissions, according to official smog test results, wins the "Most Effluent" award.

UNDER THE FLAGS OF FOUR COLONIAL POWERS

Which four nations?

Monterey's human story began thousands of years ago when nomadic hunter-gatherers discovered the area's bountiful natural resources. Their way of life changed forever after maritime explorer Sebastián Vizcaino claimed the land for Spain in 1602. Vizcaino's arrival began a succession of occupation by colonial powers, making Monterey the only place in North America to have lived under the flags of four nations.

Don Gaspar de Portola arrived in 1770 to establish a permanent Spanish presence in Monterey. Privateer Hippolyte Bouchard sailed into the bay in 1818 to claim the land for Argentina. Unable to find support for his cause, he burned the presidio and departed empty-handed. The territory declared allegiance to Mexico in 1822

A CONVOLUTED HISTORY

WHAT: History told in words and pictures

WHERE: Monterey State Historic Park

COST: Free

PRO TIP: For the Monterey Harbor text, look for a tall, abstract pelican sculpture mounted on a heavy rock pedestal.

During the 2018 renovation of the Monterey Conference Center the *Monterey Mural* was removed tile by tile, stored away, and then re-installed on the new building.

Top: *A section of the* Monterey Mural *on the rear wall of the Conference Center*

Inset: *The Monterey Harbor monument near Fisherman's Wharf*

on that nation's independence from Spain. Concerned by threats of annexation by British forces, US Navy Commodore John Sloat seized control from Mexico in 1846.

You can read this convoluted history engraved on a marble slab near the entrance to Fisherman's Wharf under the title *Monterey Harbor*. For those who prefer to absorb their history visually, a 45-foot by 11-foot glazed-tile mosaic *The Monterey Mural* by Guillermo Wagner Granizo tells the same story in colorful, cartoon-style vignettes, covering the period from Rumsen village communities to bustling Cannery Row. The mosaic is mounted on the rear wall of the Monterey Conference Center, opposite Casa Soberanes at 336 Pacific Street.

21

WEIRD, WONDERFUL, AND OBSCURE ARTISTS

Where can I see their work?

A mild climate, colorful history, scenic coastline, and easy-going lifestyle encouraged an influential art colony on the Monterey Peninsula in the late 1800s. Monterey museums and city buildings hold collections representing styles that emerged from that beginning, from tonalism to impressionism and beyond. Following are weird, wonderful, and obscure aspects of local art on public display.

Spanish émigré Salvador Dalí (1904–1989) ranks high on the scale of weird and bizarre. One of the 20th century's most celebrated surrealist masters, he fled Spain in 1940. His nearly eight years in the area are best remembered for a 1941 Surrealist Party at the Hotel Del Monte. The Monterey History and Art Association's Salvador Dalí Exhibition at 5 Custom House Plaza displays etchings, lithographs, and sculptures.

In the wonderful category, the Monterey Museum of Art (MMA) has a rich collection of early Californian paintings. Many works feature scenes and landscapes executed on the Monterey Peninsula. Armin Hansen (1886–1957) painted striking images of fishermen at work. Gottardo Piazzoni (1872–1945), who when asked his religion, replied, "I think it is California," is represented by four early modernist landscape murals originally painted for the old San Francisco Main Library.

MONTEREY'S BEST

WHAT: Monterey Museum of Art

WHERE: 559 Pacific St.

COST: Adults $15, 18 and under free

PRO TIP: MMA plans to vacate the downtown facility and move to 720 Via Mirada. Check status before visiting.

Weirdness in the Salvador Dalí Exhibition gallery

Twenty-two works by influential female impressionist E. Charlton Fortune (1885–1969) illustrate local scenes as well as scenes from England and France.

Francis McComas (1874–1938) may be obscure today, but according to the *Los Angeles Times*, in 1923 he was "rated among the 20 best painters of the world." In 2021, the MMA presented the first retrospective of McComas's work since 1939 under the title "Rediscovering California's First Modernist." His iconic *Cypress, Monterey* is at the MMA. Other works hang in the Inn at Spanish Bay and Herrmann Hall of the former Hotel Del Monte.

E. Charlton Fortune signed her work using only the initial of her first name, Euphemia, to hide her gender from prospective buyers. Her paintings sell for over a million dollars today.

23

FEATHERED PENS AND HARD BEDS

Why is it called the birthplace of modern California?

Appointed Alcalde (mayor, judge, and tax collector) of Monterey after the US seized California from Mexico in 1846, Navy chaplain Walter Colton set out to build a town hall and schoolhouse. He financed the project by taxing "sinful malefactors," including gamblers, liquor store owners, and inebriated citizens. He sentenced serious offenders to terms of construction labor. Built from locally quarried stone, Colton Hall's New England-style architecture contrasted with contemporary adobe structures. "It's not an edifice that would attract any attention among public buildings in the United States, but in California, it is without rival," wrote Colton. When it was completed in 1849, visitors hailed Colton Hall as the largest and most impressive public building west of the Mississippi.

Colton Hall, California Historical Landmark #126, is called the birthplace of modern California for its role in hosting the state's first constitutional convention in 1849. The constitution document drafted there featured progressive articles on suffrage, women's property rights, and the prohibition of slavery. The upper floor museum recreates a scene of long tables scattered with quill-feather pens and unfinished documents, as if awaiting the delegates' return from a break in negotiations.

It took a year of debate and dispute before Congress agreed to welcome California as the 31st state on September 9, 1850.

WHAT: Colton Hall Museum and Old Monterey Jail

WHERE: 570 Pacific St.

COST: Free

PRO TIP: Public entrance to the Old Monterey Jail is from Dutra Street at the rear of the building.

Top: *Detail from Colton Hall Museum*

Inset: *The jail entrance*

An attached single-story building served as the city jail until 1956. Peek into each of the dark, heavily-barred cells to see sleeping cots, guitars, and artifacts associated with real and fictional inmates. Recreating a scene from Steinbeck's *Tortilla Flat*, "Danny's cell" portrays a blanket-covered figure huddled on a bunk. No one ever escaped from this solid, granite-block-walled fortress.

LEGEND OF THE SHERMAN ROSE

Did General Sherman jilt Senorita Bonifacio?

American sea captain John Rogers Cooper arrived in Monterey in 1823. He married Incarnación, General Mariano Vallejo's sister, and became a Mexican citizen in order to own property. Over many years and ownership changes, his walled, two-acre Cooper-Molera holding expanded to include two adobe houses, barns, a cookhouse, and a warehouse. In 2019, the National Trust for Historic Preservation restored the complex for a museum and retail and event space.

Within the compound, an orchard garden includes almond, fig, pear, walnut, and apple varieties that would have been available in Cooper's time. A climbing Tea-Noisette rose, *Chromatella*, grows against the wall. Also known as the "Sherman Rose," this pale-yellow bloom is associated with a popular legend of the late 1800s. Union General William Tecumseh Sherman served as a lieutenant in Monterey from 1846 to 1847. The legend tells that the young lieutenant presented a cutting of a rose to the beautiful senorita Maria Ignatia Bonifacio and promised to return to wed her by the time it took root and bloomed. Instead, in 1850 he married the daughter of a prominent politician in Washington and never returned to Monterey.

SHERMAN'S ROSE

WHAT: Cooper Molera Adobe and Garden

WHERE: 506 Munras Ave.

COST: Free to enter the gardens, donation appreciated for museum entry

PRO TIP: The Alta Bakery in the Cooper-Molera building serves freshly baked breads, cakes, tarts, and an "elevated New American menu."

Top: *The Cooper-Molera orchard*

Inset: *Senorita Bonifacio's rose arbor, circa 1916*

According to rosarians, the first cuttings of the rose, then known as "Cloth of Gold," did not arrive in Monterey until 25 years after Sherman left, but, fueled by an energetic promoter, the fable drove a boom in yellow roses and quaint tearooms. Senorita Bonifacio's black-clothed presence and rose-covered arbor outside her adobe home on Alvarado Street became a tourist landmark. In the early 1920s, artist Percy Gray moved the Bonifacio Adobe and the rose to a new site at 785 Mesa Road, where it is called the Sherman Rose Cottage.

Fanny Van de Grift Osbourne was living in the Bonifacio Adobe in 1879 when the lovesick Scottish author, Robert Louis Stevenson, arrived to pursue her affections.

27

UNDER THE INFLUENCE OF SATAN

Why did Robert Louis Stevenson start a forest fire?

Lovesick and almost penniless, 29-year-old Scottish author Robert Louis Stevenson arrived in Monterey in late 1879 in pursuit of Fanny Osbourne, whom he had met in France. While awaiting Fanny's divorce (they eventually married in San Francisco in 1880), he loved to walk and hiked rugged Point Lobos south of Carmel, claimed by some as the inspiration for landscape features in his novel *Treasure Island*. Stevenson had suffered from a chronic lung ailment since childhood and fell seriously ill while exploring on horseback in Robinson Canyon (in today's Santa Lucia Preserve). Finding the author close to delirium, goat rancher Jonathan Wright ministered to him for two weeks until he had recovered sufficiently to travel.

On his return, Stevenson stayed at Manuela Perez de Girardin's two-story, stone, and adobe lodging house, then

STEVENSON'S SHENANIGANS

WHAT: Robert Louis Stevenson's activities in 1879

WHERE: 530 Houston St.

COST: Free

PRO TIP: The Stevenson House is open to the public on Saturdays from 10 a.m. to 4 p.m.

Louis: Is it Lewis, or Louie? He was christened Robert Lewis Balfour Stevenson. He dropped the Balfour and changed the spelling of Lewis to the French form, but retained the English pronunciation.

Top: *The Stevenson House*

Inset: *An engraved portrait of Stevenson after a drawing by Fanny Osbourne on display in the building.*

called the French Hotel. He made friends with a group of local bohemians and wrote essays and notes for *The Amateur Emigrant*, a travelogue of his arduous sea and rail journey from Scotland. He described his adventures on the Monterey Peninsula in the story, "The Old Pacific Capital." California Historical Landmark #352, now known as the Stevenson House, exhibits a collection of furniture, photos, and family items. Members of the R L Stevenson Club of Monterey continue to celebrate the life and promote the work of the author.

With great remorse, in a letter to a friend, Stevenson wrote that while walking in the forest near Pacific Grove he became curious as to whether the green moss (lace lichen) dangling from pine trees burned easily. He lit it. It did. As he explained: "I must have been under the influence of Satan. . . . Yesterday I set fire to the forest, for which, had I been caught, I should have been hung out of hand to the nearest tree. I have run repeatedly, but never as I ran that day."

AND NOW
THERE ARE TWO

Who stole Dennis the Menace?

During his early career at Disney, cartoonist Henry (Hank) Ketchum worked on many imaginary characters, including Bambi, Donald Duck, and Pinocchio. But he drew his most beloved creation, Dennis the Menace, from real life. Ketchum's wife, Alice, burst into his Carmel studio one afternoon in 1950. She shouted, "Your son is a menace!" Instead of napping, four-year-old Dennis had wrecked his bedroom. In a classic example of turning lemons into lemonade, Ketchum started drawing. A freckle-faced legend was born. Within a couple of years, newspapers carried the adventures of the lovable imp to an estimated 30 million readers across the world.

In 1988, Ketchum commissioned Academy Award-winning animator Wah Ming Chang to create a bronze statue of Dennis the Menace for installation at the entrance to the children's playground in Monterey's El Estero Park. The three-foot-tall, 200-pound Dennis joined attractions that included a huge, black, 1924 steam locomotive, a climbing wall, a suspension bridge, slides, swings, and other imaginative play structures. As children entered the park, they rubbed his big toe to a shine for luck.

The Vasquez Adobe at 546 Dutra Street (the original Dennis's new location) is the birthplace of outlaw folk-hero Tiburcio Vásquez, also branded as a menace in his time.

DISAPPEARING DENNIS

WHAT: Comic strip character

WHERE: 777 Pearl and 546 Dutra Sts.

COST: Free

PRO TIP: Climbing on the locomotive, one of the long-time favorite attractions of the park, is no longer permitted for safety reasons.

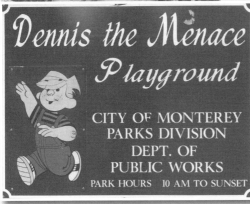

Top: *The original bronze casting now at the Vasquez Adobe*

Inset: *Image of a menace recognized around the word*

In 2006, Dennis disappeared. City officials offered a $5,000 reward for the statue's return. After receiving no response, they installed a replacement. Ten years later, Dennis turned up at a scrapyard in Orlando, Florida. The scrapyard owner's daughter-in-law recognized the cartoon figure. Her Internet search revealed that the statue had been stolen. The city honored the reward, and Dennis came home to Monterey. After minor restoration work, the original Dennis now stands outside the city's recreation administrative offices at the Vasquez Adobe. The perpetrators are still at large.

THINGS THAT GO BUMP IN THE NIGHT

Was Dr. Stokes a murderer?

Visions of Old Monterey invoke glamorous balls, fiestas, dashing Spanish horsemen, and guitars strummed by romantic suitors, but stories of intrigue, murder, and business scams also abound. Not surprisingly, these regrettable incidents have generated an abundance of grisly ghosts, haunted houses, and specter sightings.

Author Randall Reinstedt and tour operator Gary Munsinger have established themselves as local tellers of tales from this dark past. Munsinger shares his stories while driving his Ghost Tour of Old Monterey trolley, decorated with zombie masks and skeletons. Reinstedt has published more than two dozen local history books, bearing such titles as *Ghostly Tales* and *Mysterious Happenings of Old Monterey*. Both men are celebrated purveyors of the paranormal and take delight in embellishing legends of dastardly deeds and things that go bump in the night, especially those perpetrated at the haunted Stokes Adobe, which has housed a succession of popular restaurants. This notoriety did not deter celebrity diners, including Bob Hope, Dean Martin, and Frank Sinatra.

Sailor James Stokes jumped ship in the 1830s. He established a pharmacy and practice as "Dr." Stokes with a chest of purloined nautical medical supplies in a two-story

STOKES SURGERY

WHAT: Two-story 1833 adobe

WHERE: 500 Hartnell St.

COST: Free to view from the street

PRO TIP: A casual restaurant featuring tapas/small plates called Stokes Adobe now occupies the historic building.

Top: *Dr. Stokes's adobe today*

Inset: *There's even a Stokes' Ghost wine label.*

adobe built in 1833. His lack of medical training may have contributed to the 1835 death of Jose Figueroa, the Mexican governor of Alta California. Even though other patients died under mysterious circumstances, Stokes prospered and married the widow of one of them. Afflicted with alcoholism and diminished capacity in 1864, Stokes killed himself with a lethal dose of strychnine. His ghost has been sighted on the stairs by several visitors. Scheid Vineyards makes a Petite Sirah varietal described as "Just what the doctor ordered" under the "Stokes' Ghost" label. Other characters move items around and tap on walls.

Hattie Gragg, who is identified as one of the ghosts, owned Stokes Adobe when John Steinbeck visited to hear tales of paisanos, who appeared as characters in *Tortilla Flat*.

33

A BLUEPRINT FOR ROCK FESTIVALS

Who clashed with The Who?

Advertisements summoning the young people of California to a three-day concert in 1967 urged them to "Be happy, be free, wear flowers, bring bells." Tickets cost $2.50, $4.50, and $6.50. Pioneering festival promoter Lou Adler persuaded more than 30 bands to perform for free. All proceeds went to charity. Held at the County Fairgrounds from June 16 to 18, the Monterey International Pop Festival served as the template for a generation of future events, notably Woodstock. An estimated 200,000 attended over the three days, and the "Summer of Love" was born.

The concert delivered many significant firsts in the history of popular music. The Who made its first major US appearance here. Jimi Hendrix, Otis Redding, Ravi Shankar, and singer/trumpeter Hugh Masekala made debut performances before a predominantly white audience. Other acts included the Byrds, Eric Burdon & the Animals, the Grateful Dead, Janis Joplin with Big Brother & the Holding Company, and Simon & Garfunkel.

With both the Jimi Hendrix Experience and The Who eager to make their mark, the two bands argued over who would be first to astound the audience with their guitar-destroying displays. After a coin toss, The Who went first. Following

POP PYROTECHNICS

WHAT: Site of the 1967 music festival

WHERE: Monterey County Fairgrounds, 2004 Fairground Rd.

COST: Fee to enter depends on the event

PRO TIP: Limited parking is available at the fairgrounds. Check for convenient, event-related transportation from Monterey Peninsula College.

Left: *The Jimi Hendrix mural by Hiero Veiga and Thomas "Detour" Evans is on Redwood Avenue in Sand City.*

Right: *A poster lists a who's who of 1960's rock.*

a frenetic performance of "My Generation," Pete Townshend destroyed his guitar and, accompanied by explosions and smoke bombs, jammed its neck into an amp. Hendrix's performance is rock legend. Determined to go one better, he ended his set by pouring lighter fluid on his guitar and setting it ablaze. The cremains sold at auction for $375,000 in 2012. Hendrix is memorialized on a giant mural in Sand City. D. A. Pennebaker's documentary movie *Monterey Pop* (1968), which features Hendrix's pyrotechnics, raised the event to mythic status across the world.

The fairgrounds have been home to the annual, three-day Monterey Jazz Festival since 1958.

MONTEREY'S MOON TREE

What is a Moon Tree?

Monterey's Friendly Plaza is home to two curiosities with moving histories. One, of wood, traveled hundreds of thousands of miles to put its roots down here. The other, of stone, just a few feet.

While Apollo 14 astronauts Alan Shepard and Edgar Mitchell walked on the moon in February 1971, command module pilot Stuart Roosa orbited above them, carrying seeds of five species of native American trees. To study the effects of weightlessness on germination and growth, on their return to earth the US Forest Service distributed seedlings for planting in parks, schools, and government offices across the country. Known as the Moon Tree, a coast redwood (*Sequoia sempervirens*) seedling planted next to the Bertold Monument in Friendly Plaza thrived and now towers over the park.

German immigrant George Bertold prospered as a Monterey shoe-store owner. After he died in 1909, he left money to beautify the Colton Hall grounds. In 1914, Arthur Putnam, sculptor of the Lower Presidio Park's Sloat Monument, executed a stone memorial designed by noted San Francisco architect Willis Polk. Placed directly in front

NASA did not keep track of Moon Tree planting locations, but former astronaut David Williams tracked down 80 of the sites. Although 21 had died, the causes appeared to be unrelated to their time in space.

The Moon Tree shades the Bertold Monument.

SELENIC SEEDLING

WHAT: Redwood tree from seeds that orbited the moon

WHERE: Friendly Plaza, 570 Pacific St.

COST: Free

PRO TIP: Don't miss Colton Hall Museum and Old County Jail, just a few steps away.

of Colton Hall, the tall pedestal is flanked with ornate, twisted columns and topped by a large urn. The pedestal face is inset with a bronze bas-relief of two cougars and an inscription of a romantic Victorian poem mythologizing the charms of the old Spanish capital. Because the monument blocked the view of Colton Hall, the city moved it across to Friendly Plaza in the 1950s, where it now stands in the shade of the Moon Tree.

STAIRWAY TO HUCKLEBERRY HEAVEN

What is a wildlife guzzler?

From the summit of the 81-acre Huckleberry Hill Nature Preserve, pine-shaded trails offer tantalizing glimpses of the distant, ocean-blue palette of Monterey Bay. But getting there takes some effort.

Locals call the stairway access up Presidio View Trail from Veterans Memorial Park "the Stairway to Heaven." Runners describe it as "the kind of place you go to if you really want to feel some pain . . . in a good way." A 300-foot elevation gain up 184 (185 if you count the lower landing) wooden railroad-tie steps, followed by a final short burst up an even steeper dirt section, is rewarded with a choice of trails under a canopy of tall, native Monterey pines.

On Summit Trail, near the peak of the hill, the city has installed a 550-gallon water station to serve wildlife during the dry season. Called a guzzler, the design provides easy

STRESSFUL STAIRS

WHAT: Steep stairway climb to pine-shaded hiking trails

WHERE: Huckleberry Hill Nature Preserve

COST: Free

PRO TIP: Enter on Veterans Park Trail from the parking lot at the top of Veterans Memorial Drive.

Do not confuse this city preserve with Huckleberry Hill, Point of Interest #2 on 17-Mile Drive in Pebble Beach.

Left: *The exercise . . .*

Inset: *. . . and the reward*

access to water without the danger of animals falling in and drowning. Trails named Bear Track, Opossum, and Wild Boar offer clues as to the local species.

Less active types, more interested in harvesting huckleberry-laden bushes cloaking the forest understory, can relax at strategically placed rest platforms on the way up the stairs. Huckleberries are tiny and laborious to harvest, but the reward of homemade huckleberry pie makes the climb and the effort worthwhile. Peak huckleberry season is July through September.

SLOAT'S SAD EAGLE

Why is his monument crowned with a drooping eagle?

With Monterey Bay in the background, an imposing monument in Lower Presidio Historic Park celebrates Commodore John Drake Sloat's seizure of Monterey for the US from Mexican authorities in 1846. The monument is built on a pedestal of quarried stone blocks inscribed with the names of donating organizations, and its unique dimensions are replete with symbolic references. The base is 24-feet square, representing the hours of the day; the base stones are four feet long, equal to the number of hours in a sailor's watch. The 13-foot-high pedestal is a reference to the original 13 colonies that formed the United States, and the total height of 31 feet corresponds to California's entry as the 31st state of the Union.

Dedicated at a grand ceremony in July 1910, the monument is crowned by a giant eagle. The 1906 earthquake destroyed the original planned figure, a statue of Sloat pointing to the American flag at the Custom House, by sculptor Arthur Putnam. Short of funds and time to recreate that figure, the monument committee selected the eagle from the artist's surviving statuary. The solution generated an unfortunate match; the bird's crouching stance conflicts with the proportions of the pedestal, resulting in a sad, drooping appearance.

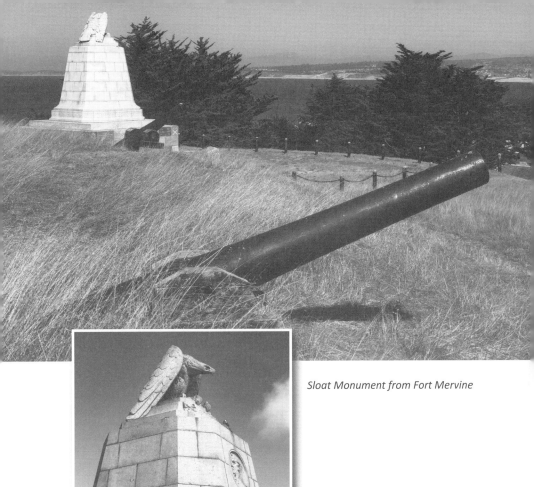

Sloat Monument from Fort Mervine

The Lower Presidio Historic Park is leased from the army by the city for public recreation. A battery of cannons remaining from its service as Fort Mervine stand guard behind the monument. The fort was the first American fort on the West Coast and was named for the captain who led the landing force.

A paved Americans with Disabilities Act (ADA) pathway enables wheelchair access up steep Vista Trail to the monument, allowing a view of the harbor and bay.

"THE CITY WILL BE REDUCED TO CINDERS"

Why does the flag of Argentina fly over Monterey?

Captain Hippolyte Bouchard, a French-born naval commander of the new republic of Argentina, saw himself as a patriotic leader of revolutionary forces fighting the country's former colonial master, the King of Spain. Authorized as a privateer to plunder Spanish ships and ports, in November 1818 he sailed two armed vessels with a force of 400 men into Monterey Bay. Bouchard demanded "the surrender of your city with all the furniture and other belongings of the King. If you do not do so, the city will be reduced to cinders."

Spanish Governor Pablo Vicente de Solá's refusal to negotiate culminated in a barrage of cannon fire from both sides. The Spanish gunners critically damaged one of his ships, but Bouchard landed troops near Pacific Grove and attacked from the rear. By then, Monterey's inhabitants had evacuated inland to safety. Unable to find any civilians to convert to the anti-Spanish cause, Bouchard looted and set fire to presidio buildings and departed, empty-handed, six days after raising the flag. This incident is the only documented land-to-sea battle on the West Coast of the US.

PLUNDERING PRIVATEER

WHAT: Monument commemorating the 1818 Argentinian attack on Spanish Monterey

WHERE: Lower Presidio Historic Park, enter at Pacific Street and Artillery Road.

COST: Free

PRO TIP: The Bouchard monument and flag are located on the Harbor Trail with a Serra monument and other historic information panels.

Left: *Howard Burnham portrays Bouchard in a 2018 reenactment of the Argentine invasion.*

A granite monument placed in the Lower Presidio Historic Park by an Argentinian organization in 1979 bears a bronze plaque titled La Armada Argentina. Look for the blue and white colors of Bouchard's adopted country waving from the monument's flagstaff.

The Presidio of Monterey Museum in the park relates its history from the indigenous period up to its current role as an army training base and language school.

MAKK RUKKAT

Do you speak Rumsen?

Several hundred people living in five villages scattered across the Monterey Peninsula and Carmel Valley spoke the Rumsen (also spelled Rumsien and Rumsian) indigenous language at the time of Spanish colonization. The Spanish called them "Costanoan" or "Coast people." These local Rumsen speakers were one of the many Ohlone tribes, numbering around 15,000 people, whose territory extended north to the San Francisco Bay Area. Eight separate languages (not dialects), as different from one another as Spanish is from French, were in use across this region. Isabel Meadows, the last native Rumsen speaker, died in 1939.

Text on an interpretive sign titled, "We live. We are here" on the Harbor Trail in Monterey's Lower Presidio Historic Park, describes the clothing, domestic duties, and basket-making skills of a typical Rumsen woman. The title is translated into her language as "*Makk rukkat. Chiyya makk rottey.*"

RUMSEN ROCKS

WHAT: Indigenous peoples' artifacts

WHERE: Lower Presidio Historic Park

COST: Free

PRO TIP: Find the ADA-accessible Harbor Trail near the lower parking, across from the Presidio of Monterey Museum.

The Costanoan Rumsen tribe has over 2,000 members who honor their cultural heritage through annual gatherings and programs to reclaim their language.

Top: *The Rain Rock*

Inset: *Acorn mortars in Lower Presidio Historic Park*

The Rain Rock, a large boulder on the hill above the Presidio of Monterey Museum in the park, is evidence of indigenous presence on this site for thousands of years. The rock is indented with 43 cup marks or cupules. Although ground into the rock surface in the same manner as traditional mortars for grinding acorn meal, their size and placement indicate a different function. Historians speculate that they served a ritual purpose associated with the weather or ceremonies related to seasonal fishing and hunting activities. Two traditional acorn mortars are set low in the grass near the fence overlooking the harbor.

BLESSING OF THE FLEET

What is a lampara net?

Fishermen fleeing hard times in Sicily's Palermo Province thrived in Monterey after Pietro Ferrante's 1905 introduction of lampara nets sparked a boom in the sardine canning business. Although women were not welcome on the boats, they played important roles on land where, as biologists, fish cutters, laborers, and business managers, they kept the canneries humming and profitable for nearly 50 years.

Ferrante's descendants and many other Sicilian families dedicated a monument to "those who made their living from the riches of the sea" on a pier at the end of Old Fisherman's Wharf.

Jesse Corsaut's bronze statue *The Fisherman* depicts a worker hauling a sardine-laden net.

With one of the most concentrated Sicilian communities in the US, the residential area on the slope above Monterey is known as Spaghetti Hill. The immigrants introduced many cultural and religious ceremonies from their homeland.

Monterey's Japanese community operated about 20 percent of the fleet. Learn about their fishing heritage at the Japanese American Citizens League Heritage Center, 424 Adams Street.

*Monuments to Monterey's
fishing heritage*

One of these, the Monterey Fisherman's Festival, is organized by
the Festa Italia Foundation every September. The event embraces
the observance of the Feast of Santa Rosalia, the patron saint of
Palermo, and the Blessing of the Fleet. High mass sung in San Carlos
Cathedral is followed by a procession to the wharf for a priest's
blessing of the fishing vessels and rededication of a statue of Santa
Rosalia overlooking the harbor.

THE JAZZ BUS

Why are those buses covered in cartoons?

To promote ridership, Monterey Salinas Transit (MST) introduced a bus rapid transit line in 2012 and named the new route JAZZ. MST conceived JAZZ as a lower-cost alternative to building a light-rail system to speed public transportation in a heavily trafficked corridor by building queue jump lanes and giving traffic-signal priority to buses.

Riders travel in bold jazz-themed vehicles that have reduced travel time by up to 25 percent along the route from the Monterey Bay Aquarium and Cannery Row through downtown Monterey and Seaside to the major shopping center in Sand City. Global positioning system-enabled electronic passenger information signage provides real-time information on bus arrival schedules. These and other JAZZ features make staying in lower-cost accommodations along the route convenient and eliminate searching for expensive parking near popular visitor attractions.

Brazilian illustrator Pablo Lobato painted high-energy, cartoon-style images for the buses. Custom boarding shelters designed in association with the Monterey Jazz Festival create a linear museum that stretches over the seven-mile route and highlights some of the most outstanding performances at the annual event. Each shelter features photographs, text, and music from a different year's artist or band. Access to the musical performance is from the rider's smartphone and QR codes displayed on the shelters.

ALL THAT JAZZ

WHAT: JAZZ public bus transportation

WHERE: Between Cannery Row and Sand City, CA

COST: Primary fare is $2.50, discount is $1.50

PRO TIP: Two JAZZ routes, A and B, operate at approximately 30-minute intervals. Check the MST website for current schedules.

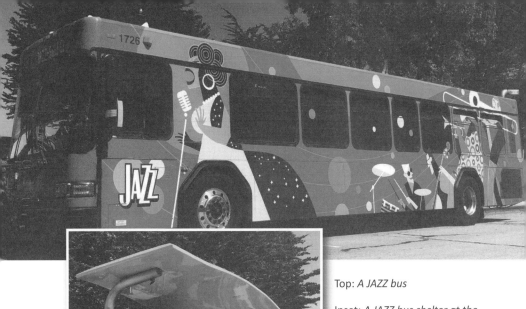

Top: *A JAZZ bus*

Inset: *A JAZZ bus shelter at the Monterey Bay Aquarium stop on Cannery Row*

The initial shelter presentations focused on the first 30 years of the festival through legendary musicians, including Dave Brubeck, Miles Davis, Ella Fitzgerald, Dizzy Gillespie, and Herbie Hancock. In celebration of the festival's 60th anniversary in 2021, MST revamped the exhibits to showcase a new generation of performers from recent festivals, featuring Terence Blanchard, Diana Krall, Joshua Redman, and Esperanza Spalding.

Even if you are not waiting for a JAZZ bus, you can listen to music from MST's Jazz Archive at mst.org/jazz.

THE QUEEN OF AMERICAN WATERING PLACES

How did a navy base catalyze California art and tourism?

The Hotel Del Monte thrived as one of the nation's first major resort destinations. Built by Charles Crocker and his railroad-baron associates in 1880, the hotel proved popular with wealthy and influential guests from President Theodore Roosevelt, Andrew Carnegie, and Joseph Pulitzer to artists, poets, writers, and Hollywood movie stars. They enjoyed its 20,000 acres of gardens, golf course, polo grounds, and race track, and took carriage rides along 17-Mile Drive. Fire destroyed the hotel twice—first in 1887 and again in 1924. A third, Spanish-Revival-style incarnation continued the hotel's reputation as one of the world's showplaces until it was purchased by the US Navy for use as a training base in 1947. The reception and former public areas of the hotel are now Herrmann Hall, the Naval Postgraduate School's administrative center.

In addition to being a catalyst for the county's hospitality industry, the hotel helped establish the market for Californian art. A gallery opened in 1907, showcasing artists displaced from San Francisco by the earthquake. Featuring work by the royalty of early California painters, Charles Rollo Peters, William Keith,

POSTGRADUATE ART

WHAT: Herrmann Hall

WHERE: Naval Support Activity and Naval Postgraduate School, 1 University Cir.

COST: Free on occasional public open days

PRO TIP: The general public can reserve a table for brunch in the Barbara McNitt Ballroom on the last Sunday of each month. Call 831-656-7512 at least two weeks prior to the desired date.

Top: *The Hotel Del Monte, now (2012) as Herrmann Hall on a public open day*

Inset: *The Hotel Del Monte (circa 1930)*

Arthur Mathews, Gottardo Piazzoni, Xavier Martinez, Eugen Neuhaus, and Will Sparks, the gallery won wide acclaim and strengthened the region's growing reputation as a center for plein air landscape painting.

After the fire of 1924, the hotel commissioned large artworks to decorate public spaces. Noted artists Ferdinand Burgdorff, Daniel Sayre Groesbeck, and Francis McComas contributed paintings. Murals by Moira Wallace adorned the Bali Room walls and Jo Mora sculpted La Novia, a glass-encased diorama of an early California wedding party. Some of their works still decorate Herrmann Hall.

The former hotel guest room wings are open to military personnel and their families as a facility of the Monterey Navy Gateway Inns & Suites (NGIS) service.

A CORNUCOPIA OF THE WORLD'S FLORA

What is an Arizona garden?

Railroad baron Charles Crocker, owner of Monterey's Hotel Del Monte, planned for the gardens and grounds of his "Queen of American Watering Places" to be a key attraction for his guests. In 1881 he hired German-born architect Rudolf Ulrich to landscape the 127-acre site. Ulrich created walks and carriage drives lined with ornamental trees and shrubs through the natural oak and pine forest cover. Flower beds close to the hotel displayed 90 varieties of roses and other plantings in "a cornucopia of the world's flora." Unique features of the grounds included an Arizona garden, a cypress-hedged "Mystic Maze," and Laguna del Rey, a lake that remains visible to the public through a fence along Del Monte Avenue.

An exotic, desert-themed Arizona garden became the crown jewel of the hotel's landscaping attractions. With a crew of eight men, Ulrich scoured desert territories served by his employer's railroad system and returned with several boxcar-loads of cacti, many of them up to 10 feet high. A short stroll from the hotel, he created a symmetrical design of raised beds outlined with shells and rocks. Plantings of over 60 cacti species were augmented with agaves, aloes, yuccas, palms, and ornamental grasses.

The garden remained a popular photo opportunity for guests until the US Navy purchased the land in 1947.

Ulrich created other Arizona gardens in California, including at the Palo Alto Stock Farm owned by Crocker's railroad partner, Governor Leland Stanford, now the campus of Stanford University.

CACTUS BED DEL MONTE

Top: *The Arizona garden (circa 1900)*

Bottom: *The Arizona garden now*

After years of neglect and alterations, including a road cut through one edge, Naval Postgraduate School (NPS) volunteers began restoring the garden in the early 1990s. The public is admitted only in the company of military personnel, on occasional campus open days, or when attending a public Sunday brunch.

CRAZY FOR CACTUS

WHAT: Exotic Victorian cactus garden

WHERE: Naval Support Activity and Naval Postgraduate School, 1 University Cir.

COST: Free

PRO TIP: Diners attending Sunday brunch at Herrmann Hall can stroll through the garden. Call 831-656-7512 at least two weeks prior to the desired date.

PATHS OF HISTORY

Do you prefer the long or the short tour?

Monterey's downtown Path of History connects more than 50 sites related to the city's heritage. Start your self-guided tour of Monterey State Historic Park at the Pacific House Museum on Custom House Plaza, then follow a series of round, yellow tiles set in the sidewalk. They will lead you to some of California's oldest adobe buildings, including several that played a role in Monterey's transition from a remote Spanish outpost to US statehood. Highlights of the tour include the Custom House, California's first theater, Colton Hall, Larkin House, Stevenson House, and the Royal Presidio Chapel.

If you haven't the time or the energy for the full Path of History walk, 35 rectangular bronze plaques embedded in a brick pathway at the entrance to Colton Hall offer a condensed version of the story. Beginning with recognition of Native Americans as the "The Ancient Ones," the plaques progress through "Chinese Fishermen (1851), the artists of

---

HISTORY AFOOT

WHAT: Walking tours of Monterey history guided by plaques set in the sidewalk

WHERE: The tour begins at the Pacific House Museum. The short walk is at Colton Hall.

COST: Free

PRO TIP: Monterey has preserved more original Mexican-era adobes than any other city in California.

Monterey State Historic Park visitors may take a cell phone tour of historic downtown buildings by dialing (831) 998-9458.

Left: *Bronze plaques in the Colton Hall entrance walkway*

Right: *A yellow tile that marks the Path of History trail through downtown.*

"Bohemian Monterey" (1874), and "Italian Fishermen" (1875), to the Hotel Del Monte, which established Monterey's role as a world-class tourist destination.

A circular bronze bas-relief of the Great Seal of the State of California adopted at the state Constitutional Convention held at this site in 1849 is set at the head of the walkway. The Great Seal of the State of California holds 31 stars representing the State's order of admission to the union. The state motto, Eureka, meaning "I have found it," lies below the stars.

"MR. GORBACHEV, TEAR DOWN THIS WALL"

Why are pieces of the Berlin Wall at the Presidio?

One of the most familiar and symbolic artifacts of the Cold War, the Berlin Wall fell in 1989. The wall's demise culminated in the toppling of the East German regime, the reunification of Germany, and, in 1991, the collapse of the Soviet Union. Sensing a business opportunity, Phoenix, Arizona hotel tycoon Irvin Dyer purchased three 12-foot-high concrete slabs of the wall for $110,000 in 1990 and stored them in a warehouse.

Several years later, Walter Scurei, who as a child in Berlin had witnessed refugees fleeing the Red Army, discovered the slabs abandoned in the warehouse. He paid the outstanding storage fees and erected them in his garden, where they became a local attraction.

On a visit to Phoenix, Skip Johnson, a deputy inspector general at the Defense Language Institute Foreign Language Center (DLIFLC) at the Presidio of Monterey, saw Scurei's display

---

BERLIN BARRIER

WHAT: Berlin Wall Memorial

WHERE: On the campus of the DLIFLC, Presidio of Monterey

COST: Free; access is restricted to employees of DLIFLC and their guests.

PRO TIP: For public access to the Presidio, watch for occasional open tours of DLIFLC.

Sections and fragments of the Berlin Wall are in private and public collections around the word, including the International Spy Museum in Washington, DC.

"Dedicated to those who fell"

and learned that he was interested in donating the slabs to an educational institution. Johnson arranged for them to be moved to Monterey. In 2005, the Institute installed the three segments as the Berlin Wall Memorial in the Language Day quad near the Korean Department of the language school. The text on the memorial plaque states:

"Dedicated to those who fell trying to reach freedom.
Those who fell preserving freedom, and
All who served defending freedom."

FIRST CATHEDRAL

Is it a chapel or a cathedral?

Designed by the Academy of San Carlos in Mexico City and constructed by local indigenous labor in 1794, the Royal Presidio Chapel is the first-known architecturally designed stone building, the oldest continuously functioning church, and the first cathedral in the state of California. It is also the only structure remaining inside the limits of the original presidio walls. After the Mexican government took over the missions, the chapel became Monterey's Catholic parish church until elevated to the role of San Carlos Cathedral in 1850.

A square, two-story, conical, tiled-roof bell tower on the northeast corner flanks an ornate, Moorish-influenced facade embellished with decorative niches, pilasters, and scrollwork. The oldest non-indigenous image sculpted in California, a bas-relief rendering of Our Lady of Guadalupe, is mounted near the apex of the ornamental arch. Conservators restored the figure and surrounding rays to remove damaging salts and evidence of previous efforts during a major restoration of the cathedral in 2009.

Massive wooden doors swing open to reveal a classic, high-ceilinged, basilica-style nave. Transepts added in 1858 resulted in the present cross-shaped floor plan. A lattice pattern painted on the interior walls is interspersed with bunches of grapes in the rich gold, green, and red colors of Spain.

SACRED ART

WHAT: Former Royal Presidio Chapel

WHERE: 500 Church St.

COST: Free

PRO TIP: Archaeological items recovered during restoration work are displayed in the adjacent Royal Presidio Chapel Heritage Center.

Stone carving of Our Lady of Guadalupe on the façade of San Carlos Cathedral

Sections of the wall plaster have been removed to expose a monochromatic-gray version of an original pattern from the Mexican era. The Stations of the Cross were painted in Rome in the late 19th century for Holy Cross Church in Santa Cruz and were donated to San Carlos in 1953.

San Carlos Cathedral is the venue for twilight chamber concerts of baroque music performed on period instruments during the annual Carmel Bach Festival.

SECRET GARDENS OF OLD MONTEREY

Where are the quietest gardens?

Monterey State Historic Park comprises some of the best-preserved Spanish, Mexican, and early American buildings in the West. Nine of them have gardens that the park website describes as the "Secret Gardens of Old Monterey." Some contain fountains where you can make a wish. Others have arbors and walkways bordered by abalone shells or wine bottles. They come in sizes from a few planters to a few acres. Heavy gates and high stone walls around the following gardens isolate them from much of the urban bustle and noise.

White stucco walls enclose the Pacific House Memory Garden (20 Custom House Plaza), which once hosted bull and bear fights for cheering crowds. Landscape architect Frederick Law Olmsted Jr. redesigned the space as a courtyard for more tranquil pursuits in 1926. Shaded by southern magnolia trees set around an octagonal, raised pool and fountain, the garden is a popular venue for local celebrations.

A stout wooden gate set in an archway through a tile-capped stone wall opens to the Larkin House Garden (464 Calle Principal). The first and only US Consul to Mexican California, Thomas Larkin, built his two-story, whitewashed adobe home in 1835. Beginning in the 1920s,

Local building materials combined with the French-inspired, Carolina-style balconies of the Larkin House became the prototype for the popular Monterey Colonial residential architectural style.

Top: *The Sherman Quarters in the Larkin Garden*

Inset: *A fountain in the Pacific House Memory Garden*

GATED GARDENS

WHAT: Walled gardens open to the public

WHERE: Downtown Monterey

COST: Free

PRO TIP: Look out for other public buildings on the Monterey Path of History with gardens open to the public. The three noted above are the author's favorites.

his granddaughter developed an English cottage-style garden in the rear, walled area. A one-room, stone veneer adobe cottage abutted to the garden wall served as quarters for Lt. William T. Sherman during his service in California.

Scottish author Robert Louis Stevenson lived at the Stevenson House (530 Houston Street) for several months in 1879. In the 1920s and '30s the owner transformed the barren, dry patch behind the former hotel into an intimate garden, with winding paths and densely planted beds of cineraria, foxgloves, and poppies.

SECRET KILLERS

What is whale breaching?

Secret Killers of Monterey Bay, a video produced by the National Geographic Society, documents research on killer whales in Monterey Bay from 1990 to 2000. Killer whales (*Orcinus orca*), commonly called orcas, are the largest species in the dolphin family. They are highly intelligent, live in complex social structures, and are considered the ocean's apex predator. Even great white sharks steer clear of them. Marine biologists categorize orcas into resident and transient categories.

Residents typically remain in local waters and feed primarily on fish, especially salmon. The southern resident population of Monterey Bay and the waters of the Big Sur coast has shrunk to under 100 in recent years, due to a decline in Chinook salmon and other environmental factors. Transient orcas range in deeper, distant waters and are distinguished by having more pointed fins and saddle patches. They prey on marine mammals, such as gray whales, dolphins, and sea lions. In the spring, packs of gray whales cross the mouth of the bay on their annual migration from the Gulf of California to Alaska. Transient orcas stalk them for their newborn calves.

From spring through fall, humpback whales move into the bay following seasonal shoals of anchovies and krill. To the delight of viewers on the shore, they often display their

---

All dolphins are whales, but not all whales are dolphins. Dolphins are toothed members of the whale order (*Cetacea*) and are smaller than the baleen or "great" whales.

Top: *A breaching humpback whale.*

Inset: *Two orcas hunting.*

Photos courtesy of Linda Abbey

acrobatic breaching behavior while feeding close to land. Breaching is when a humpback whale leaps out of the water while slapping its fins and flukes on the surface.

Arriving in the summer, blue whales typically cruise farther from shore at a sedate five miles per hour. At up to 100 feet long and weighing as much as 200 tons (equal to 30 elephants), they are the largest mammals on earth. Other regular visitors to the bay include smaller dolphins, porpoises, sharks, and giant ocean sunfish (mola molas).

DEATH STALKS THE DEEP

WHAT: Marine mammals of Monterey Bay

WHERE: Best viewed from commercial whale-watch cruise boats

COST: Check on local operators' websites

PRO TIP: Cruises operate from Monterey and Moss Landing harbors. Reservations are recommended.

SECRETS OF THE OCEAN

Do they have a great white shark?

Exhibits with a secret theme are popular at the Monterey Bay Aquarium. Opened in 1988, "Mexico's Secret Sea," the first exhibit to present live animals not necessarily found near Monterey, featured marine life from the Sea of Cortez and drew large crowds. More recent titles include: "Liquid Luminous Secrets" (artwork in association with the Jellies exhibit), and "The Secret Lives of Seahorses." Be sure to check the schedule for future "secret" installations.

With over 200 exhibits and 80,000 plants and animals, the Aquarium opens a window onto a fish's-eye view of the secrets and wonders of Monterey Bay and beyond. Sway with the movement of a two-story-tall kelp forest bustling with fish and cavorting sea otters; stand in the middle of a school of endlessly circling sardines; or look up into a million-gallon tank of barracuda, sunfish, and tuna at the county's most popular indoor attraction. You can sign up for

FISH'S EYE VIEW

WHAT: An undersea view of the marine life of Monterey Bay

WHERE: 886 Cannery Row

COST: $34.95 to $49.95, children 4 and under are free

PRO TIP: It's fun to watch the otters being fed. Check feeding times and arrive early to beat the crowd.

Monterey is the only known aquarium to have displayed great white sharks for up to six months. They were returned to the ocean after they grew too big to keep safely.

Denizens of the deep

text message alerts of UFOs (unscheduled feeding opportunities) and unusual wildlife sightings from the ocean-view outside decks.

The Aquarium is involved in many aspects of marine life beyond public exhibits. Staff scientists work to rebuild sea otter populations, protect California's ocean, and transform fisheries and aquaculture worldwide. Policy experts help to draft and implement legislation to address climate change and end plastic pollution. The Seafood Watch Program provides recommendations to consumers and restaurants for seafood that's fished or farmed in environmentally sustainable ways.

TAKE THE CHICKEN WALK

Who was Bruce Ariss?

The Bruce Ariss Way staircase is a shortcut from Wave Street down to Cannery Row and the Aquarium. The stairs replace the "Chicken Walk," a steep, wooden-plank boardwalk with cleats similar to ladders used in chicken coops that cannery workers took as a shortcut to get to work. A mural by John Cerney on the rear of the building where Ariss Way crosses the former Southern Pacific railroad track shows a group of laborers who served as models for *Mack and the Boys*, characters in Steinbeck's story who climbed the walk to reach the Palace Flophouse.

THE SETTING FOR THE STORIES

WHAT: The heart of Steinbeck's Cannery Row

WHERE: Wave Street and Irving Avenue

COST: Free

PRO TIP: Ed Ricketts's laboratory, the model for "Doc's" Western Biological, is across the road, at 800 Cannery Row.

Nearby, three wooden cabins that formerly housed Filipino, Japanese, and Spanish families indicate the ethnic diversity of the cannery workforce.

Ariss, a free-spirited artist, writer, and associate of Steinbeck and marine biologist Ed Ricketts, painted a whimsical mural panel mounted at the foot of the stairs. His

Each cannery had its own unique steam whistle sound to summon the workforce. Housed in the former Hovden Cannery, the Aquarium continues to sound its whistle daily at noon.

Left: *Ariss mural with Corsaut bust of Kalisa Moore at the base of the stairs*

Inset: *Cerney's mural of workers who served as the models for* Mack and the Boys *overlooks the Monterey Bay Coastal Recreational Trail.*

rendering portrays a vacant lot where discarded cannery boilers housed homeless families in *Sweet Thursday*, the sequel to *Cannery Row*. Flora Woods's Lone Star Café, shown on the left side of the picture, operated until 1941, when California Attorney General Earl Warren ordered all brothels closed.

Next to the mural, sculptor Jesse Corsaut's bronze bust depicts Kalisa Moore, the "Queen of Cannery Row" and former owner of Kalisa's La Ida Café, a popular bohemian gathering place in the late 1950s. The Wing Chong Building, next to the café, with its distinctive, overhanging second-story balcony, served as the model for the "Heavenly Flower Grocery," Lee Chong's "miracle of supply" for Old Tennis Shoes whiskey (guaranteed four months old) and other necessities of life on the Row.

HOLLYWOOD AND FISH HOPPERS

What was Marilyn Monroe doing on Cannery Row?

Since Thomas Edison's cameraman captured flickering movie moments at the Hotel Del Monte Hotel in 1897, filmmakers have favored the Monterey Peninsula for movie settings. Cannery Row has starred in several Hollywood epics. With scenes shot at the Sardine Factory restaurant, perhaps most famous is Clint Eastwood's directorial debut, *Play Misty for Me*.

Fritz Lang's 1952 noir classic *Clash by Night* introduced a then-little-known (other than to the citizens of Castroville, see page 10) Marilyn Monroe to the world as a fish cutter. In one scene, she emerges from a cannery building and walks across the street with her co-star, Paul Douglas. Filmed from this very same spot but after the cannery was razed, the opening credits of Nick Nolte's 1982 interpretation of "Doc" in the movie version of John Steinbeck's *Cannery Row* roll over a view of the bay.

FISHY STORIES

WHAT: Hopper used to transfer fish to the cannery

WHERE: 484 Cannery Row

COST: Free

PRO TIP: For more movie information, see the "Hurray for Hollywood" interpretive panel in the sidewalk.

Monterey Boat Works, now converted to an auditorium on the campus of Stanford University's Hopkins Marine Station, built many of the hoppers.

Top: *Fish hopper amid derilict cannery foundations*

Bottom: *The Fish Hopper restaurant on the pier*

Crumbling foundations and rotting pilings, gritty skeletons from Cannery Row's past, still haunt this stretch of the waterfront. A wooden fish hopper stranded in a dystopian landscape of concrete and twisted rebar is an artifact from cannery owner Knut Hovden's 1927 introduction of purse-seine fishing nets. The earlier bucket-and-cable transfer method of landing the catch could not keep pace with a vastly expanded harvest, so he designed a floating craft called a hopper to hold and pump fish ashore through underwater pipes.

THE GHOST RAILROAD

Is there anything left to see?

The railroad's arrival in 1874 drove rapid growth of Monterey's fishing and tourism industries. Popular with wealthy San Franciscans traveling to the Hotel Del Monte, the Del Monte Express was Southern Pacific's longest-running, named passenger train. Although the last locomotive departed from Monterey in 1979, ghosts of the "glory days of steam" remain scattered along the railroad right-of-way.

Today, jingling bicycle bells replace hissing steam along the 18-mile stretch of the Monterey Bay Recreational Trail (the "Rec Trail" to locals), laid over the former Southern Pacific route from Castroville to Pacific Grove. Rusting tracks parallel the trail through Fort Ord Dunes State Park as far as Seaside. In 2021, Handcar Tours started offering a Kalamazoo handcar experience on a six-mile stretch of the tracks through Marina.

In Monterey, the Dust Bowl Brewing Company Tap Depot occupies the former depot at 290 Figueroa Street. On the

Travel by train from San Francisco to Monterey in the Victorian era was often quicker, and surely less stressful, than via today's crowded freeways.

Left: *The peak of Monterey's railroad era*

Inset: *The nadir of Monterey's railroad era*

rear side of a warehouse behind 275 Cannery Row, a colorful mural by artist John Cerney celebrating the railroad depicts workers loading sardine crates into a boxcar. Where Drake Avenue crosses the trail, railroad signaling equipment and a memorial bust of Ed Ricketts mark the site of his fatal collision with the Del Monte Express. A boxcar that at one time served as a bookstore stands about 1,000 feet further west.

An unimproved dirt path, still owned by Union Pacific as the successor to Southern Pacific, passes behind residential neighborhoods on the west side of Pacific Grove. A concrete culvert embossed with the 1915 construction date, wooden railroad ties upended for bollard posts, and glimpses of steel tracks embedded in tarmac remain as mementos. A replica of a Greek-cross-style passenger shelter that served visitors to the Asilomar YWCA Leadership Camp in the 1930s stands near Dennett Street.

GREAT PARTIES AT THE LAB

Who was John Steinbeck's best friend?

Unless you are on a Steinbeck Country pilgrimage, you will likely pass by Pacific Biological Laboratories unaware of its historical connections. This two-story, weathered wood structure, the model for "Doc's" Western Biological in *Cannery Row*, is where marine biologist Ed Ricketts developed his theories of marine ecology and processed specimens for the Smithsonian and museums and schools across the country. It also served as a gathering place for artists and writers, including Joseph Campbell and Henry Miller. In "About Ed Ricketts," a eulogy to his best friend and collaborator, Steinbeck recalled "Great parties at the laboratory."

A fire that started in the adjacent Del Mar Cannery burned Ricketts's original lab to the ground in 1936. With financial help from Steinbeck, Ricketts rebuilt the structure and it resumed its role as a center for bohemian intellectual and social life. For many years after his death in 1948, the lab operated as a private men's club and the high jinks continued. Today, the lab is owned by the City of Monterey and is occasionally open for public tours. You can view concrete tanks that held marine specimens at the rear of the lab from a walkway alongside the Clement Hotel.

RICKETTS ON THE ROW

WHAT: The former Pacific Biological Laboratories

WHERE: 800 Cannery Row

COST: Free on public open days

PRO TIP: Check the City of Monterey Museums, Pacific Biological Laboratories webpage (monterey.org/museums/City-Museums/Pacific-Biological-Laboratories) for open days.

Left: *Front entrance to Ed Ricketts's Pacific Biological Laboratories*

Bottom: *Specimen holding tanks at the rear.*

Half a mile away, at the corner of Wave Street and Drake Avenue, a memorial to Ricketts overlooks the spot where he died after his old Buick sedan stalled on the railroad crossing ahead of the oncoming Del Monte Express train. Visitors frequently place cut flowers in the hand of the bronze bust of Ricketts by sculptor Jesse Corsaut.

Ricketts delivered the manuscript for *Between Pacific Tides*, his handbook on intertidal life, to Stanford University Press just days before the fire that destroyed his lab. The book is one of Stanford's best-selling titles.

TED'S DREAM

Who is the madam portrayed in this sculpture?

Life-size bronze castings of four "boys" seated on a rocky ledge celebrate the group of entrepreneurs who engineered the rebirth of the canning district based on hospitality and tourism.

Ted Balestreri, the founding visionary of the Cannery Row Company, dreamed of creating a monument to inspire visitors with their story. Ted's dream, together with a million dollars in donations, resulted in *The Cannery Row Monument*, a bold portrayal of real and fictional characters who contributed to the blend of colorful stories of hard work, legend, and fantasy that created Cannery Row.

This dominating sculpture on Steinbeck Plaza comprises nine bronze figures by Carmel sculptor Steven Whyte, perched on a 15-foot-high granite boulder. The four seated entrepreneurs are Ted Balestreri, Bert Cutino, Harry Davidian, and George Zarounian. John Steinbeck looks down from the peak. Around the base are figures of a Chinese fisherman, marine biologist Ed Ricketts inspecting a specimen

---

THE BOYS WHO REBUILT THE ROW

WHAT: *The Cannery Row Monument* sculpture

WHERE: Steinbeck Plaza, Cannery Row and Prescott Avenue

COST: Free

PRO TIP: Ted Balestreri and Bert Cutino's Sardine Factory restaurant appeared in *Play Misty for Me*, Clint Eastwood's movie directorial debut.

Enclosed bridges over Cannery Row are crossovers that carried cans of sardines from the canning operation to warehouses. Today, they serve as pedestrian walkways.

Top: *Balestreri and the boys on the monument*

Inset: *Steinbeck bust*

of Monterey Bay tide-pool sea life, and the infamous "madam" Flora Woods with one of her "girls." Steinbeck used Ms. Woods, the real owner of a house of ill repute in the 1930s, as inspiration for Dora Flood in his novels *Cannery Row* and *Sweet Thursday*.

Nearby, an earlier bust of Steinbeck stands above a plaque inscribed with the first paragraph of *Cannery Row* and one of the most famous opening lines in American literature: "Cannery Row in Monterey in California is a poem, a stink, a grating noise, a quality of light, a tone, a habit, a nostalgia, a dream." In *A Journey into Steinbeck Country*, Susan Shillinglaw tells how the writer's first wife, Carol Steinbeck, embittered by his desertion of her for a younger woman, encouraged the sculptor to portray his facial features in an unflattering manner.

PACIFIC GROVE'S UNDERWATER GARDENS

Where is California's only underwater municipal "garden"?

Google Maps locates Pacific Grove Marine Gardens Park at a parking turnout off Ocean View Boulevard, west of Lovers Point. Garden-loving visitors are disappointed to find a dusty bluff edge covered with yellow blooms of Hottentot fig, an invasive succulent popularly known as Caltrans' ice plant for its ubiquitous role lining freeways.

The elusive "marine gardens" are actually hidden beneath the waters of Monterey Bay immediately below the bluff. Managed by the California Department of Fish and Wildlife, Pacific Grove Marine Gardens State Marine Conservation Area is one of 124 marine protected areas (MPAs) spanning the California coastline. In the 1950s, glass-bottom boats took visitors to view the kelp forest thriving below the surface. Today, non-scuba divers can enjoy this aquatic landscape and its teeming inhabitants in the Kelp Forest exhibit at the Monterey Bay Aquarium.

Concerned by pollution from Cannery Row fish processing plants and excessive collection of marine specimens, biologists at Stanford University's Hopkins Marine Station enlisted Pacific Grove mayor Julia Platt's help to establish a refuge to protect the ocean-floor habitat. Platt led the drive for approval of an ordinance in 1932, creating a sanctuary for invertebrate

MARINE GARDENS

WHAT: Marine Protected Area of Monterey Bay

WHERE: Opposite 1235 Ocean View Blvd., Pacific Grove, CA

COST: Free

PRO TIP: Look for the parking turnout signed #3 Acropolis off Ocean View Boulevard.

Top: *A great blue heron looks out over Pacific Grove Marine Gardens.*

Inset: *The kelp forest at Monterey Bay Aquarium. Photo courtesy of FASTILY (CC BY-SA 4.0)*

marine life along the entire city waterfront to a depth of 60 feet. Pacific Grove is the only city granted the right by the state legislature to control submerged lands along its coastline. Platt's pioneering effort began a conservation movement that led to the long-term recovery of Monterey Bay.

California MPAs are designated to protect the diversity and abundance of marine life, the habitats they depend on, and the integrity of marine ecosystems.

JOHN DENVER DIED HERE

Why did his aircraft plunge into Monterey Bay?

One of the most popular singer/songwriters of the 1970s, John Denver, died when his aircraft plunged into Monterey Bay. A memorial plaque mounted on a boulder on Ocean View Boulevard overlooks the windy spot in the Pacific Grove Marine Gardens State Marine Conservation Area where the plane crashed into the water. The closing verse from "Windsong" is inscribed on the plaque:

> "So, welcome the wind and the wisdom she offers,
> follow her summons when she calls again.
> In your heart and your spirit, let the breezes surround you.
> Lift up your voice then and sing with the wind."

Born Henry John Deutschendorf Jr. in 1943, Denver recorded numerous multimillion-selling hits, including "Take Me Home, Country Roads" and "Rocky Mountain High." He supported many environmental and humanitarian organizations and cofounded the Windstar Foundation wildlife preservation agency and the World Hunger Project. Denver was an enthusiastic aviator who logged over 2,700 hours in the air and earned pilot ratings for single-engine, multi-engine, glider, and instrument flying. He also worked with NASA to promote the "Citizens in Space" program and in 1985 passed NASA's rigorous physical exam, putting him in line for an early space flight. Sadly, he did not live long enough to take advantage of that opportunity.

FATAL FLIGHT

WHAT: Small, bronze memorial plaque mounted on a rock

WHERE: Opposite 1275 Ocean View Blvd., Pacific Grove, CA

COST: Free

PRO TIP: Look for parking turnout signed #4 Asilomar.

Top: *Rutan Long-EZ N3R. Photo NOAA public domain image.*

Inset: *The John Denver memorial plaque*

On October 12, 1997, Denver flew a Rutan Long-EZ experimental, lightweight plane from Monterey Peninsula Airport out over the bay. Low on fuel and unable to reach the auxiliary tank switch, he crashed into the Marine Garden waters a few hundred yards offshore. He died instantly.

Denver's aircraft joined 463 other vessels recorded as wrecked in the chilly waters of the Monterey Bay National Marine Sanctuary since 1841.

SUMMER PLACES

Where did that beach come from?

A Summer Place, one of 1959's most popular movies, takes place on Pine Island off the coast of Maine. Starring teenage heartthrobs Sandra Dee (as Molly) and Troy Donahue (Johnny), the movie also starred two unique area residences. The LaPorte Mansion in Pacific Grove played the role of the Pine Island Inn where the lovers meet, and the Walker House in Carmel was the home of Molly's on-screen parents.

The LaPorte Mansion, a grand, 1895, Queen Anne-style, gabled and turreted residence, formerly known as the Pinehurst Mansion, sits at the rear of a six-acre corner lot shaded by Monterey pines. A gazebo built by the film crew still stands near the driveway entrance. When the movie camera pans across the scene to establish the inn's oceanside setting, it settles on a flight of stairs leading down to the water. This juxtaposition is an illusion of the silver screen—in reality, the ocean is nearly a mile away, and the beach is not visible from that point.

The Walker House setting required no such cinematic sleight of hand. Mrs. Clinton Della Walker told iconic American architect Frank Lloyd Wright, "I want a house as durable as the rocks and as transparent as the waves." So, he squeezed her single-story, 1,200-square-foot home onto a narrow granite promontory projecting into Carmel Bay like the prow of a ship.

Built in 1952 of mellow local stone and covered by a broad, copper roof finished with blue-green shingles, the house has a

Recorded by the Percy Faith Orchestra, the instrumental "Theme from A Summer Place" spent nine weeks at number one on the Billboard Top 100 chart in 1960.

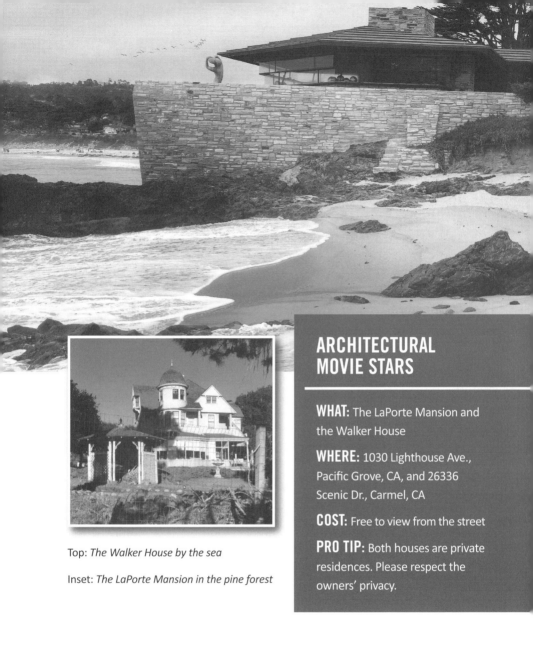

Top: *The Walker House by the sea*

Inset: *The LaPorte Mansion in the pine forest*

WHAT: The LaPorte Mansion and the Walker House

WHERE: 1030 Lighthouse Ave., Pacific Grove, CA, and 26336 Scenic Dr., Carmel, CA

COST: Free to view from the street

PRO TIP: Both houses are private residences. Please respect the owners' privacy.

hexagonal floorplan oriented to fit the triangular site. There isn't a square corner in the house. Mrs. Walker's "cabin on the rocks" was Wright's final California architectural commission and his only oceanfront home. Although hidden behind high gates, its dramatic profile is visible to all from the public beach.

THE SOCIALITE KEEPER

Who was Emily Fish?

Placed into service on February 1, 1855, Point Pinos is the West Coast's longest continuously operating lighthouse. Alcatraz Island Lighthouse preceded Point Pinos by eight months, but was decommissioned in 1909 due to expansion of the prison. The City of Pacific Grove now owns the site and manages docent tours, but the US Coast Guard continues to service the light.

Two female lightkeepers managed Point Pinos lightstation in the early days. The first keeper, Charles Layton, died after he was shot chasing an outlaw as a member of a sheriff's posse. His wife, Charlotte, succeeded him from 1856 to 1861. Appointed in 1893, Emily Fish served until 1914. Known as the "Socialite Keeper," she frequently entertained guests for afternoon tea.

Ms. Fish's log provides fascinating insight into her era. She hired more than 30 men and fired most of them for incompetence. Her April 18, 1906 entry on the San Francisco earthquake notes, "At 5:13 A.M., violent and continued earthquake shocks jarred the lens, causing it to bend the

---

TECHNOLOGY AND TEA

WHAT: Operating lighthouse and museum

WHERE: 98 Asilomar Blvd., Pacific Grove, CA

COST: Access to grounds is free; fee to tour the interior

PRO TIP: Be sure to watch the short video of the lighthouse story in the basement.

Between 1896 and 1934, nine ships were wrecked near Point Pinos, none of them because the light was not functioning.

Top: *The lighthouse*

Inset: *The lighthouse's longest-serving keeper, Emily Fish*

connecting tube and loosened the lens. Telegraphic and telephonic communication obstructed beyond Salinas and Pajaro—track obstructed—no trains. Del Monte Hotel wrecked by falling chimneys, two guests killed."

Guided by original drawings and permits, Heritage Society of Pacific Grove volunteers have performed extensive restoration on the building. The original Fresnel lens, manufactured in France, remains in place. Successive generations of illumination technology have fueled the light, from whale and lard oil to kerosene, incandescent vapor, and electricity. The current automated light source is a permanently illuminated, 1,000-watt bulb amplified by the lenses to produce a 50,000-candlepower beam visible up to 17 miles at sea. If a lamp burns out, a spring flips a new lamp into position.

COOL CRITTERS OF THE CALIFORNIA CURRENT

Who painted whimsical sea creatures on a federal building?

Alaskan artist Ray Troll is known for blending art and science into fishy images that swim into museums, books, magazines, and onto T-shirts worn around the world. In 2009 he created 32 whimsical images of stylized sea creatures he called *Cool Critters of the California Current* for a mural on the National Oceanic & Atmospheric Administration (NOAA) Southwest Fisheries Science Center laboratory in Pacific Grove. Roberto Salas and Guillermo Jauregui reproduced them on six-foot by eight-foot fabric panels using acrylic paint.

Each panel's background color illustrates how fish, marine mammals, sea turtles, and other fauna have responded to changing ocean conditions. Other panels depict ships and technologies used by the fishery's scientists and innovations in fishing vessels and gear employed over the decades. The 400-foot-long mural wraps around the exterior of all four sides of the bland, concrete structure, which was originally built to house a US Navy radar facility. Funded by a NOAA grant to preserve the department's history, they are adhered to the upper level to create a crowning fresco.

NOAA personnel at the laboratory moved to Santa Cruz in 2015. Admirers of Troll's colorful designs are concerned

COOL CRITTER WHIMSY

WHAT: Wraparound mural of stylized ocean creatures

WHERE: 1352 Lighthouse Ave., Pacific Grove, CA

COST: Free to view from the street

PRO TIP: "Blue Seas and Green Seas," an online art exhibit of the Pacific Grove Museum of Natural History, includes many of the images Troll created for the mural.

Thirty-two fishy images wrap around the former NOAA laboratory.

that the federal government will sell the site to developers, who could demolish the building and the mural. A group of community leaders and scientists are pursuing efforts to acquire the building and transform it into a Center for Ocean Art, Science, and Technology (COAST).

Troll's mural serves as a convenient aiming point for golfers on the 15th hole of the Pacific Grove Golf Links.

THE GREAT TIDE POOL

What is a sneaker wave?

John Steinbeck based the character of "Doc" in his 1945 novel *Cannery Row* on the personality of his marine biologist friend Ed Ricketts. On several occasions, Steinbeck helped Ricketts collect marine specimens at a spot near Point Pinos that they called The Great Tide Pool. When, in the story, Doc gathers starfish at the site, Steinbeck describes it as "a fabulous place when the tide is in, a wave-churned basin, creamy with foam . . . But when the tide goes out the little water world becomes quiet and lovely."

The Great Tide Pool Trail is a short stretch of the California Coastal Trail within the Asilomar State Marine Reserve. An interpretive sign advises, "Tide pool creatures are very fragile and easily damaged by our feet. Seaweeds are also very slippery. The best way to enjoy the tide pools is to wait quietly and watch them come alive." Beware that taking or possessing tide pool animals in a Marine Protected Area is against the law. Also watch for sneaker waves—never turn your back to the ocean.

WAVE-CHURNED BASIN

WHAT: A crescent-shaped rocky tide pool with a sandy beach

WHERE: Sunset Drive, Pacific Grove, CA, north of the junction with Lighthouse Avenue

COST: Free

PRO TIP: Look for a colorful interpretive panel on the bluff overlooking the tide pool.

Sneaker waves are large swells that surge high up the beach without warning. Every year, unsuspecting beachcombers are dragged into the water and drown.

The Great Tide Pool

"It is a fabulous place: when the tide is in, a wave-churned basin, creamy with foam... But when the tide goes out the little water world becomes quiet and lovely. The sea is very clear and the bottom becomes fantastic with hurrying, fighting, feeding, breeding animals."
- John Steinbeck, *Cannery Row*

Tide pool creatures are very fragile and easily damaged by our feet. Seaweeds are also very slippery. The best way to enjoy the tide pools is to wait quietly and watch them come alive.

"A fabulous place when the tide is in."

Ed Ricketts explored tide pools from Alaska to Mexico, searching for specimens for his Pacific Biological Laboratories business and for insight into the relationships between all living things. His classic marine biology work, *Between Pacific Tides*, written together with John Calvin, is one of the best-selling books published by Stanford University Press. Eric Enno Tamm wrote in *Beyond the Outer Shores*, "Arguably more than any scientist of his time, Ed Ricketts saw the tide pool as the place where celestial and worldly forces interacted most vividly."

"THE CITY WILL BE REDUCED TO CINDERS" (page 42)

A MISSION, A HACIENDA, AND A HAUNTED FORT (page 180)

CAME OTHER SHIPS

FROM MANY LANDS

STEAM AND IRON

WERE IN THEIR CARGO

UNDER THE FLAGS OF FOUR COLONIAL POWERS (page 20)

THE GHOST RAILROAD (page 70)

MILITARY MEMENTOES (page 14)

THE GREATEST MEETING OF LAND AND WATER IN THE WORLD (page 160)

GRAFFITI PORTAL TO THE PARK (page 12)

"FOR ENTERTAINMENT, WE HAD THE LIBRARY" (page 124)

WEIRD, WONDERFUL, AND OBSCURE ARTISTS (page 22)

SECRETS OF THE OCEAN (page 64)

J'S BUTTERFLY HOUSE (page 114)

PACIFIC GROVE'S UNDERWATER GARDENS (page 76)

TAKE THE CHICKEN WALK (page 66)

THE MAGIC CARPET AT PERKINS PARK (page 106)

WORLD'S WORST CAR SHOW (page 18)

BE HERE WHEN IT HAPPENS (page 182)

THE MAGIC CARPET AT PERKINS PARK

Who was Hayes Perkins?

Gardener and self-styled adventurer Hayes Perkins transformed a poison oak-covered ocean bluff in Pacific Grove into a dazzling springtime carpet of fluorescent-pink blooms. Photographs in *Life* and *National Geographic* magazines, as well as a giant photograph by Kodak in Grand Central Terminal, New York, enticed visitors from across the globe. One of the most loved and distinctive horticultural features of the Pacific Coast, the park continues to bring joy to all, but its creator is all but forgotten.

Henry Hayes Perkins (1874–1964) worked his way around the world as a manual laborer for 50 years, including eight years in Africa and nine at Hearst Castle, before retiring to Pacific Grove in 1938. While living in a tiny cabin overlooking Monterey Bay at Lovers Point, in 1943 he began to clear, plant, and hand-water the coastal bluff with a mix of shrubs and Mediterranean-climate succulents,

MAGIC CARPET

WHAT: Public oceanside garden of brilliant, colorful blooms

WHERE: Coastal bluff west of Lovers Point, Pacific Grove, CA

COST: Free

PRO TIP: The pink blossoms are typically at their peak in early May.

Rosea is a non-invasive succulent ground cover recommended by the California Invasive Plant Council. It is unrelated to the Hottentot fig invasive ice plant used to stabilize soil along highways.

Top: *More than 70 years after Hayes Perkins created his oceanside garden, it remains the city's most popular visitor attraction.*

Inset: Eden *cover photo, courtesy of California Garden & Landscape History Society*

predominantly pink-blooming rosea ice plant (*Drosanthemum floribundum*). Over the next 14 years, Perkins single-handedly created this one-mile-long linear garden, known to many as the "Magic Carpet."

Named Perkins Park by the city in 1950, the garden plays an essential role in the town's appeal as a resort destination, but decades of municipal financial woes led to deterioration of his legacy. Recent new resources committed by the city and volunteer Friends of Perkins Park are committed to restoring the Magic Carpet for future generations to enjoy.

HIDDEN TREASURES OF THE MUSEUM

Why are they kept in the basement?

Founded in 1883, with its genesis as a Pacific Coast branch of the Chautauqua movement, the Pacific Grove Museum of Natural History is a living field guide to the native plants, animals, geology, and cultural history of the Central Coast. Chautauqua was a popular adult education and social movement in the late 19th and early 20th centuries. Permanent public exhibits include Monterey County bird and monarch butterfly galleries, as well as special displays devoted to Pacific Grove's Chinese fishing village and local Native American baskets.

Artifacts donated over the years that no longer reflect the museum focus on local natural history are stored in the basement archives. Occasional tours downstairs reveal unique treasures, such as a collection of Southwest indigenous pottery with examples from the Anasaz, Mogollon, Hohokam, Kayenta,

BURIED TREASURE

WHAT: Museum artifacts

WHERE: Museum of Natural History, 165 Forest Ave., Pacific Grove, CA

COST: $8.95 for adults; reduced for youth and military

PRO TIP: Many of the "hidden" treasures a can be viewed on the museum's online database, pgmuseum.pastperfectonline.com.

Sandy, a life-size, anatomically correct gray whale sculpture by Larry Foster, traveled the nation for a decade before finding a permanent home in front of the museum in 1981.

Top: *Museum treasures from the Acoma Pueblo. Photo courtesy of Pacific Grove Museum of Natural History*

Inset: *Sandy, a life-size, 40-foot-long sculpture of a gray whale by Larry Foster is a favorite with visiting children*

Hopi, and Acoma people. Other items include Native American basketry, pottery and textiles from other states, a two-person Chinese gun, a Japanese pillar clock, a Haida cedar-bark chest, and a selection of Inuit bone and stone tools.

The annual Wildflower Show is a treasure that, while not hidden, is seen for only one weekend every year. Organized by the California Native Plant Society in April, it features more than 700 varieties plucked from the wild throughout Monterey County. This annual display at the museum vies with Australia's Ravensthorpe Show for the title of the world's largest.

"MUCH BAGGAGE IS NOT DESIRABLE"

What does Asilomar mean?

The first woman to earn a civil engineering degree at University of Calfornia, Berkeley, the first to practice as a professional architect in California, and renowned as the designer of Hearst Castle, Julia Morgan also created the heart of Asilomar State Beach and Conference Grounds. Thirteen of the buildings she designed between 1913 and 1928 for a YWCA Leadership Camp remain as meeting places and visitor lodging units.

Asilomar is the most extensive collection of Morgan's Arts and Crafts-style structures in one location. All of the buildings employ local stone and wood. Public areas such as the Social Hall, the Chapel, and the soaring ceiling of Merrill Auditorium feature exposed redwood beams and high windows to gather natural light and reveal views of the surrounding forest and dunes.

Two of the lodging units have unusual names. The Stuck Up Inn is named after a group of female college students who were hired for summer work. Advice in their employment notice suggests their privileged backgrounds: "Much baggage is not desirable. A steamer trunk or two suitcases will prove better than a large trunk." They were branded as

REFUGE-BY-THE-SEA

WHAT: Asilomar State Beach and Conference Grounds

WHERE: 800 Asilomar Ave., Pacific Grove, CA

COST: Free to visit

PRO TIP: Asilomar dining and lodging accommodations, events in the Social Hall, and 107 acres of beachfront forest and dunes are open to the public.

Top: *Julia Morgan's Social Hall*

Inset: *Recommended dress for Stuck-Ups in 1924*

"stuck-ups" after they objected to performing menial tasks. Wisely, the women changed their attitude and embraced the title. Young male workers who were notorious for raiding the kitchen for dessert were nicknamed "pie-rats." Their residence unit became known as the Pirates' Den.

The property's name is derived from the Spanish words "asilo," meaning refuge, and "mar," meaning sea. the YWCA adopted the name to promote its property as a "Refuge-by-the-Sea."

WHERE OTTERS AND WHALES PLAY IN THE PARK

Why did some locals object?

A windstorm destroyed an ancient Monterey cypress tree overlooking the bay in Pacific Grove's Berwick Park. City workers trimmed the branches but left two large stumps. John Bridges, a Monterey attorney, noticed their resemblance to breaching humpback whales. With Public Works Department permission, the Rotary Club and the Chamber of Commerce hired chainsaw artist Jorge Rodriguez in 2016 to carve the stumps into the shapes of whales. He patched areas of rotten wood with new lumber and bonding materials. Instead of finishing the sculpture with natural wood color as originally planned, Rodriguez painted the surface to hide these repairs.

Most residents enjoyed the whales as an attractive addition to the park. A vocal few did not. Saying they were more appropriate for Disneyland, they demanded their removal. Visitors love them, and today they are one of the town's most popular photo opportunities.

A less controversial marine sculpture also installed by the Rotary Club stands a short distance away. Cast in bronze by local sculptor Christopher Bell in 1994, *Life at the Top* portrays

Another tree sculpture, *Bad Day on the SS Normandie*, depicting a giant octopus attacking an ocean liner, faces onto Del Monte Boulevard at 50 Coral Street, Pacific Grove.

MARINE MAMMAL SCULPTURE

WHAT: Humpback whales and otter sculptures

WHERE: Berwick Park, Ocean View Blvd., Pacific Grove, CA

COST: Free

PRO TIP: To keep the lush lawn pleasant for picnickers, dogs are not permitted in Berwick Park.

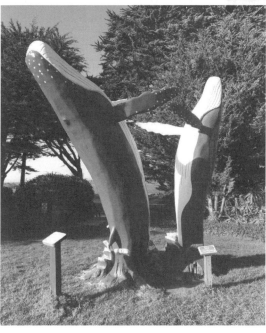

Sculptures of humpback whales and otters overlook their natural domain.

a mother sea otter cradling her pup. "I see people embracing the sculpture in sheer enjoyment," he commented. "That's great. My goal is to evoke a response." A second casting of Bell's otters is at the rear entrance to Monterey's Portola Hotel & Spa. He also created *Butterfly Kids*, a bronze statue of two children in monarch butterfly wing costumes, at the entrance to the Pacific Grove Post Office.

J'S BUTTERFLY HOUSE

Where are the butterflies in Butterfly Town?

Sonja and J Jackson (simply "J" is how he liked to be known) owned a modest bungalow on Pacific Grove's Ninth Street. Diagnosed with retinitis pigmentosa at age 18, Sonja slowly lost vision until becoming legally blind. J painted a large wooden butterfly in colors bright enough for her to see and placed it in front of their home. Seeing her delight, he added more butterflies in various colors, shapes, and sizes. Before J passed away in late 2020, he had covered the entire façade and garden of the house with his work. Visitors who learned about the Butterfly House on social media came from all over the world to view his labor of love. Sonja said: "It was his expression of himself of the beauty and how much he loved Pacific Grove."

J chose the butterfly emblem for its association with Pacific Grove. Back in the days when hundreds of thousands of monarch butterflies overwintered in the area, the city adopted the nickname Butterfly Town, USA, to promote tourism in the winter season. Monarch images became the community emblem and appeared on banners, buildings, and businesses. The city established a Monarch Grove

REQUIEM FOR A BUTTERFLY

WHAT: The Butterfly House

WHERE: 309 9th St., Pacific Grove, CA

COST: Free

PRO TIP: The Monarch Grove Sanctuary is behind the Butterfly Grove Inn, 250 Ridge Road.

The Xerces Society's 2021 monarch count for the whole of California was 1,914 monarchs—less than 0.01% of the population during the 1980s.

Hundreds of colorful butterfly sculptures cover the Pacific Grove Butterfly House.

Sanctuary, where molestation of butterflies is punishable with a $1,000 fine.

A steep decline in the Western monarch population resulted in no butterflies roosting in the sanctuary over the winter 2021 season. Unless they return, from now on you are likely to see more butterflies decorating Sonja's home than in their official refuge.

Monterey County has two other prominent "butterfly houses." Both are named for their dramatic, overhanging eaves, reminiscent of butterfly wings. Frank Wynkoop's 1951 compact, mid-century modern home is perched above the ocean at Carmel Point. Soaring rooves top a residence built by Feldman Architecture on Santa Lucia Preserve in 2012.

HE COULD HAVE BEEN BILL GATES

Did Gary Kildall miss his opportunity?

Gary Kildall, a consultant for computer chip maker Intel Corporation and a professor at the Naval Postgraduate School in Monterey, needed to access data from a floppy disk. With no standard software available for his small computer to read the data, in 1974, he wrote a program that he called CP/M (Control Program for Microcomputers) to accomplish the task.

Together with his wife, Dorothy, Kildall founded Intergalactic Digital Research, later shortened to Digital Research Inc. (DRI), which grew rapidly by selling CP/M as an operating system (OS) to start-up personal computer (PC) manufacturers in Silicon Valley.

In 1981, IBM planned to enter the PC market and visited DRI's office in Pacific Grove to negotiate the purchase of CP/M for use on their machine. When they left, Kildall believed they had reached an agreement in principle but still had to finalize details. Several weeks later, he was surprised to learn that IBM had signed a deal for an unauthorized clone (PC DOS) of CP/M from Bill Gates at Microsoft. Not wishing to litigate with an industry giant, DRI agreed to an arrangement for IBM to offer customers a choice of OS. As IBM listed DRI's CP/M at four times the price of PC DOS, most users purchased the cheaper option, and Microsoft's version of CP/M ended up dominating the market.

Before moving Microsoft from Albuquerque to Seattle, Bill Gates visited Gary Kildall and they discussed the idea of merging their companies and locating in Monterey.

DRI staff outside 801 Lighthouse Avenue, circa 1980

Photo courtesy of Tom Rolander

Industry legend tells that IBM never met with Kildall because he was "out flying" that day and therefore missed the opportunity to "be Bill Gates." The first is false—other participants have confirmed the meeting. The second conjecture is probably unwarranted—although DRI thrived for several years by contributing important software innovations, Kildall's preference for writing code and enjoying life far outweighed his desire to reign as a captain of industry.

INTERGALACTIC DIGITAL RESEARCH

WHAT: A private Victorian residence, the first corporate headquarters of DRI

WHERE: 801 Lighthouse Ave., Pacific Grove, CA

COST: Free

PRO TIP: Look for the Institute of Electrical and Electronic Engineers' (IEEE) Milestone in Electrical Engineering and Computing plaque in the sidewalk.

117

FLAGPOLE SKATER BREAKS RECORD

What is a flagpole skater?

By the early 1920s, Holman's was the largest independently operated department store between San Francisco and Los Angeles. As a publicity stunt, store owner Wilfred Holman hired a mysterious Mr. X to roller-skate on a small platform fixed to a flagpole that stood more than 100 feet above the street on the store's roof. Mr. X broke his own roller-skating endurance record by spinning around and around for 51 hours. A silent newsreel clip of his feat, headlined "Flagpole Skater starts newest silly season sport!" appeared on movie theater screens across the nation in 1932.

John Steinbeck, who at the time was living in a family cottage at 147 Eleventh Street, incorporated the stunt of "The Mysterious Mr. X" into Chapter 19 of his novel *Cannery Row*. He recounted the citizens' reactions: Mack and the boys looked up for a moment—"they couldn't see that it made much sense"—while others wondered how the skater went to the bathroom.

SKY-HIGH SKATER

WHAT: The Holman Building

WHERE: 542 Lighthouse Ave., Pacific Grove, CA

COST: Free to view from street

PRO TIP: As of this writing, one three-bedroom penthouse condominium residence remained available.

Search for "Holman's Department Store Flagpole Skater" on YouTube, and you can watch a one-minute video of the event.

Top: *Holman's Department Store in the late 1920s*

Inset: *Screen shot from the 1930 newsreel clip*

Photos courtesy of Heritage Society of Pacific Grove

Carol and John Steinbeck purchased household items and writing materials at Holman's. To save money, John bought two bottles of green ink for five cents in a sale. That ink lasted to page 167 of his handwritten pages for *To A God Unknown*. When he returned for more, the sale was over and he had to pay 10 cents per regular bottle of blue ink to complete the manuscript.

Remodeled in 2019, the Holman Building includes 25 luxury condominiums on the upper floors, a ground-floor restaurant, and a basement-level parking garage. The developer restored the facade with windows and other features to match the original detailing.

PROBING THE SECRETS OF THE SEA

What was Stanford's interest in marine studies?

Stanford University's Hopkins Marine Station is where "scientists and students probe secrets of the sea." Created in 1894 as a place for fieldwork in marine biology, Hopkins moved from Pacific Grove's Lovers Point in 1917 to an 11-acre site on China Point. Here, the third-oldest marine field station in the US and the oldest on the West Coast overlooks "a field biologist's dream spot"—the rocky shallows and tide pools of Monterey Bay. Hopkins's scientists have earned major research prizes, including the Presidential Science Award in Biology, by probing the secrets of topics from aquaculture to zoology. In collaboration with the adjacent Monterey Bay Aquarium, their research has expanded far beyond Monterey to include worldwide studies of tuna and other migratory fish.

The campus is closed to the public except for annual open houses for show-and-tell demonstrations of student projects. Members of the public are invited to evening lectures in the auditorium, the former Monterey Boat Works workshop. Recent talks invoking a "secret" theme include "The Secret Life of Great White Sharks," "Frozen Secrets: Ice Penetrating Radar," "Great White Sharks Have a Secret Cafe," and "The Secret Lives of Ocean Predators."

Stanford's first president, David Starr Jordan, studied fish at Harvard. He started Hopkins in the spirit of his mentor Louis Agassiz's pronouncement to "Study nature, not books."

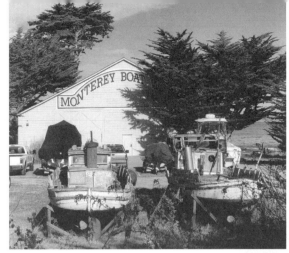

Top: *The Boat Works Lecture Hall*

Bottom: *Harbor seals resting at the Hopkins Marine Station China Cove.*

BIOLOGIST'S DREAM SPOT

WHAT: Hopkins Marine Station of Stanford University

WHERE: 120 Ocean View Blvd., Pacific Grove, CA

COST: An annual open house and some lectures are free to the public.

PRO TIP: The best public view of the seal beach is from the recreational trail opposite 187 Ocean View Boulevard.

Harbor seals have long favored secluded China Cove at the west end of the site as a safe place to haul out and relax on the beach. Groups of people gather year-round to peer at rows of sleeping pinnipeds protected behind a high wire fence. Pacific Grove erects temporary fencing along other nearby beaches to protect mother seals from harassment during the spring pupping season.

VAGRANT HOTSPOT

What is the Seawatch initiative?

With a mild coastal climate and warm inland mountain ranges offering a diverse range of habitats, Monterey is one of the nation's most bird-rich counties. Local bird-watchers have recorded close to 500 species. The Audubon Society has identified Point Pinos in Pacific Grove as one of the most important land-based observation posts for pelagic birding in North America. This rocky outcrop lies on the migratory path for many species. It also overlooks cold-water upwelling from the Monterey Submarine Canyon that supplies nutrients for fish species the birds rely on for food.

The Monterey Audubon Society sponsors an annual Seawatch initiative to count seabirds from a spot on the bluff east of Point Pinos. Every autumn, volunteer counters with telescopes are happy to talk with passersby about their observations. Typically, a chalkboard lists the current bird count and any notes on

PELAGIC POINT

WHAT: Audubon Seawatch Initiative bird-watching site

WHERE: Ocean View Avenue between Crespi Pond and Point Pinos

COST: Free

PRO TIP: See the Pacific Grove Museum of Natural History exhibit "The Amazing Adaptation of Birds," with over 400 local specimens mounted in lifelike postures.

Pelagic birds are species such as albatross, cormorants, pelicans, phalaropes, and shearwaters, that spend most of their time on the ocean away from land.

A young western gull with a passing squadron of brown pelicans near Point Pinos

unique sightings. More than 250 species have been identified here. Construction of a permanent bird observation platform near this site was approved by the city council in 2020.

Point Pinos and Crespi Pond, at the edge of the golf course, are known for a diversity of "vagrant" visitors. Vagrants are birds that have been blown off-course by severe weather, or inexperienced birds that follow routes not in their species' typical migration path. Rare sightings have included an orchard oriole, a prairie warbler, a tundra swan, and a white-faced ibis.

"FOR ENTERTAINMENT, WE HAD THE LIBRARY"

Who was entertained?

Carol and John Steinbeck lived on Eleventh Street in Pacific Grove, a few blocks away from the public library in the early 1930s. John later wrote about those penniless writing years: "For entertainment, we had the public library." Carol worked as a part-time librarian to supplement their income. Mythologist Joseph Campbell, who spent several months in the area in 1932, recalled gatherings at Ed Ricketts's Lab on Cannery Row, where participants took turns reading aloud from books borrowed from the library.

Pacific Grove's library began as a "reading corner" in a community hall in 1886. A $10,000 Carnegie grant funded a dedicated public library building that opened in 1908 with wide arches, tall, curved windows, and coffered ceilings. To meet increasing demand for services, the white stucco, red-tiled Mission-style structure was remodeled and expanded several times between 1926 and 1981. A major renovation in 2020 restored many of the interior features, including wood-framed lantern fixtures, to their original 1908 appearance.

Hayes Perkins, who created the springtime "Magic Carpet" of pink succulent blooms in Perkins Park, left his entire estate (more than $50,000 in 2020 value) to purchase books for the library in 1964. Unusual for man who worked his way around the world as a manual laborer for 50 years, Perkins wrote a 2,000-page diary of his travels, titled *Here and There*.

A CARNEGIE LIBRARY

WHAT: Pacific Grove Public Library

WHERE: 550 Central Ave., Pacific Grove, CA

COST: Free

PRO TIP: Visit the Nancy and Steve Hauk Gallery space off the reading area for changing displays of work by local artists.

Top: *A 1920s postcard view of the original library*

Bottom: *The reading area after restoration*

Self-published in a limited edition of six, his personal copy is in the library's special collection. Others are held in the archives of the Royal Geographical Society in London, the National Geographic Society in Washington, DC, and Cal Poly San Luis Obispo.

From dirt-poor kid to the richest man in the world, steel magnate Andrew Carnegie (1835–1919) funded more than 3,000 libraries in the US and overseas.

WHERE SIR FRANCIS DRAKE CLAIMED MONTEREY FOR THE QUEEN

Or was this another hoax?

With the *Golden Hind* overloaded with looted Spanish treasure in June 1579, privateer (or pirate, depending on your national allegiance) Francis Drake sought a harbor on the California coast to repair his vessel for the long voyage back to England. Most historians agree that he anchored for six weeks at Drakes Bay near Point Reyes. Drake's chaplain's diary states that before leaving to complete his circumnavigation of the globe, he left a metal plate engraved with a declaration claiming the land for England. In 1936, a brass plaque engraved with a similar text was unearthed in Marin County. However, experts claim that this plaque was a hoax.

In a similar find, a Pebble Beach resident found a barnacle-encrusted glass bottle in the sand at Moss Beach near today's Inn at Spanish Bay. When he opened the bottle in 1949, the contents, an Elizabethan sixpence coin and a tightly rolled lead scroll inscribed with a proclamation similar to the one on the Marin plaque, yielded a headline in the *Monterey Peninsula Herald* newspaper that claimed, "Discovery Here of Drake Scroll May Change Pacific History."

DRAKE'S LANDING?

WHAT: The legend of Sir Francis Drake's landing at Pebble Beach

WHERE: Moss Beach is on 17-Mile Drive at the southern end of Spanish Bay Beach.

COST: Per-vehicle charge to enter the Pebble Beach community

PRO TIP: Spanish Bay is named for the anchorage where Don Gaspar de Portola's expedition camped in 1769 while seeking Monterey Bay.

Top: *Drake's purported landing site at Moss Beach*

Inset: *The* Golden Hind *from an engraving published in 1915.*

At that time, the glass and lead tested as appropriate to the date on the scroll, but because of the Marin hoax, most authorities dismissed this local find as another counterfeit. Unfortunately, the bottle and contents vanished. The owner claimed that burglars stole them from his home. Local history buffs hold out hope that they will turn up and be validated one day.

The Marin plaque is in the collection of the University of California Bancroft Library, in Berkeley, where it serves as an object lesson in how easily such hoaxes can be accepted as facts.

NOWHERE ELSE ON EARTH

Can you trademark a tree?

The Allen Memorial Grove at Point Lobos State Natural Reserve and three Points of Interest (POI) in Pebble Beach on 17-Mile Drive south of Cypress Point are home to the Monterey cypress tree. This conifer species thrives in warm, temperate and subtropical regions worldwide, but occurs in native stands nowhere else on Earth. Widely known as *Cupresssus macrocarpa*, in 2012 UC Berkeley's Jepson Herbarium reassigned the scientific name as *Hesperocyparis macrocarpa*. New Zealanders call it Macrocarpa or simply Mac.

Crocker Grove Nature Reserve, POI #11 on 17-Mile Drive, is named for Charles Crocker, the railroad baron responsible for building the Hotel Del Monte in Monterey. A posted sign claims that the grove harbors "the largest and oldest Monterey cypress trees in existence" but fails to define "large" or give an age. Cal Poly's UFEI listing locates the "National Champion" in size 80 miles away in Pescadero, California.

Standing alone on an exposed granite outcrop overlooking the ocean at POI #12, the Lone Cypress is one of the world's most photographed trees. Scarred by fire and supported by cables, the Lone Cypress is zealously protected physically and intellectually. The Pebble Beach Company uses a silhouette

Also endemic to the region, the Monterey pine (*Pinus radiata*) is the most widely planted pine in the world. The lumber is used for building houses and as pulp for newsprint.

Left: *Crocker Grove*

Bottom right: *The Lone Cypress logo*

Top right: *A Ghost tree*

image of the tree as its logo and has threatened artists who sell artwork depicting the tree with litigation. Critics decry this as an attempt to assert trademark rights to a tree.

A cluster of gnarled, sun-bleached cypress skeletons, called The Ghost Trees at Pescadero Point, POI #13, is said to be haunted on dark, foggy nights by a willowy figure in flowing white robes. A popular Victorian tourist landmark, the Witch Tree, was lost in a storm in 1964.

CYPRESS SURVIVORS

WHAT: Groves of cypress trees

WHERE: 17-Mile Dr., Pebble Beach, CA

COST: Per-vehicle charge to enter Pebble Beach

PRO TIP: Request a copy of the 17-Mile Drive map with numbered points of interest at the entrance booths.

THE WORLD'S MOST FAMOUS AUTO BEAUTY CONTEST

What is the most expensive automobile?

It is billed as "the most famous and prestigious automobile beauty contest in the world," so the only secrets associated with the annual Pebble Beach Concours d'Elegance are on the ballots cast by the Best of Show Trophy judges. But there are plenty of surprises among the winners every year.

Since the first Pebble Beach concours in 1950, there have been coupes, convertibles, and cabriolets; saloons, sedans, and speedsters; torpedoes, tourers, town cars, and more among the winners. The oldest champion is a 1913 Rolls Royce Silver Ghost; the youngest, a 1964 Maserati Mistral Coupe. Every August, except for during the great pandemic of 2020, the 18th fairway at Pebble transforms into America's most expensive parking lot. Over the weekend of the event, more than 15,000 people squeeze onto the narrow greensward, many dressed in period costume to match their favorite automobiles, to gaze on the world's most exotic and valuable vehicles.

In 2021, the cheapest advance-purchase general admission spectator ticket cost $400. But you don't have to pay Pebble's prices to join the party. This single event has morphed into

---

The most expensive car ever sold is a 1962 Ferrari 250 GTO, which went for $48.4 million at an RM Sotheby auction in Monterey in 2018.

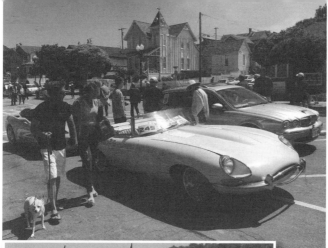

Top: *Spectators at the Pacific Grove concours event*

Inset: *Spectators at the Pebble Beach concours event. Photo by Jay Cross (CC BY 2.0)*

AUTOMOBILE ENVY

WHAT: Pebble Beach Concours d'Elegance

WHERE: 1700 17-Mile Dr., Pebble Beach, CA

COST: High

PRO TIP: When stuck in traffic that weekend, look around. You'll likely be in the company of an elegant Duesenberg or a million-dollar Ferrari.

Classic Car Week (also known as Monterey Car Week or Monterey Auto Week), when nearly 100,000 people attend more than 40 automobile-related auctions, concours, exhibits, rallies, and races across the peninsula.

For a fraction of the cheapest ticket to the Concours d'Elegance, you can show your vehicle in a judged concours event and take a rally drive through scenic Pebble Beach at the Rotary Club of Pacific Grove's annual Concours Auto Rally. Both concours organizers donate proceeds to local charities.

PLAY THE HAY

Can I really play at Pebble for under $100?

Pebble Beach is home to seven 18-hole, upscale golf courses. A round at Pebble Beach Golf Links, which claims to be "unanimously rated the number one public course in the country," costs over $600. Poppy Hills, at just $250, is definitely down-market. You must be a guest or willing to pony up membership initiation fees of more than $50,000 to step on to the greens at the private Monterey Peninsula Country Club. And it's gauche to even ask, "How much?" at Cypress Point. With only 250 members, many of whom are prominent political figures, Cypress is one of the world's most desired clubs.

If you are willing to settle for just nine holes, you can play The Hay for $65. Built in 1957 to honor former Pebble Beach head pro Peter Hay, it was one of the first par-3 courses in the country. Recently revamped with a design by Tiger Woods, The Hay is built on a slope overlooking Pebble Beach Golf Links, the site of Tiger's memorable championship performance in the 2000 US Open. The course includes an exact replica of the famed No. 7 green at Pebble Beach Golf Links, as well as holes designed to be played with any club in the bag. Unlike at most other Peninsula courses, kids are welcome to play in this no-pressure setting.

PEBBLE ON A BUDGET

WHAT: The Hay nine-hole short course

WHERE: POI #14 on 17-Mile Dr. at Portola Rd., Pebble Beach, CA

COST: $65, juniors 12 and under, free. Re-rounds, 50% discount.

PRO TIP: Snacks, souvenirs, restrooms, and free parking are available at the Pebble Beach visitor center (POI #14).

Top: *The Hay putting green*

Inset: *Richard MacDonald's* Momentum *sculpture*

Sadly, the revamp scrapped The Hay's engaging former logo, which featured Cynthia the sea lion. This cartoon character was a nod to Chief Marshal Peter Hay's assertive commands that "shook the sea lions" while restoring order to onlookers who distracted players during the 1929 US Amateur at Pebble Beach.

Momentum, a monumental bronze sculpture by artist Richard MacDonald to celebrate the 100th anniversary of the US Open Golf Championship held at Pebble Beach in 2000, welcomes players to The Hay.

BAGPIPE TRADITION ON THE LINKS

Who feared the bagpipes?

Golf began in Scotland along sandy, coastal areas called links that were of no value for agriculture. The name is derived from *hlinc*, an Old English word meaning rising ground or ridge. As sandy soil remains firm and dries rapidly, such areas became popular locations for golf courses.

PGA Tour champion Tom Watson, an honorary member of the Royal and Ancient Golf Club of St. Andrews in Scotland, was asked to consult on the design of a new, links-style golf resort at Pebble Beach's Spanish Bay. On surveying the site, a former sand mine overlooking the ocean, he said, "I can't wait to play. I can almost hear the bagpipes."

Bagpipes are the national instrument of Scotland and led generations of Highlanders into battle. Their shrill, penetrating wail terrified many an unsuspecting enemy.

MUSIC TO SOME

WHAT: Scottish bagpipe performance every evening

WHERE: Inn at Spanish Bay, Spanish Bay Dr., Pebble Beach, CA

COST: Free after Pebble Beach gate fee

PRO TIP: Check with the hotel for times, and arrive early to secure a seat.

The sound of bagpipes became so fearsome during the Highland uprisings of the 1700s that the government declared bagpipes to be a weapon. Carrying them became a penal offense.

A bagpiper entertains from tee number 2 at Spanish Bay.

To the Scottish people it is music, and playing the pipes is a tradition upheld by their descendants worldwide.

The sound of bagpipes is also a tradition at The Inn at Spanish Bay. A lone piper plays every evening to an audience enjoying cocktails on the hotel patio. Several pipers, both male and female, clad in tartan and full Scottish regalia, share the duties. Tunes range from "Scotland the Brave" to "Happy Birthday." They ask: Please don't request "Danny Boy." It's Irish.

MONTEREY JACK: CHEESE CREATION MYTHS

Who invented Monterey Jack?

Romans carried a recipe for a semi-soft Italian cheese to Missionary Father Junipero Serra's home island of Majorca. His flock adopted the process for making cheese at Carmel Mission. By the late 1800s, individuals and farmers across the region made this "Queso del Pais"-style country cheese to sell and to feed their families. That's just one of many competing stories about the origin of Monterey Jack cheese.

Scottish immigrant David Jack (he changed the name to Jacks) arrived in Monterey in 1850. By the early 1900s he owned 60,000 acres across the county. Possibly in penance for his reputation as a land shark, Jacks served as a Sunday-school teacher for 50 years and provided land for the Pacific Grove Methodist Retreat. He sold cheese as one of many products from his 14 dairy ranches. Customers called it "Monterey Jack."

THE BUSINESS OF CHEESE

WHAT: Monterey Jack cheese

WHERE: At virtually every grocery store

COST: Varies

PRO TIP: The Schoch Family Farmstead is the only Monterey County cheesemaker left making Monterey Jack cheese.

Three local parks, Jacks Park, Jacks Peak County Park, and Don Dahvee Park (the name his Mexican friends and employees called him), carry the Jacks name today.

Left: *Wheels of Monterey Jack. Photo courtesy of Schoch Family Farmstead*

Right: *David Jacks (1822–1909)*

The Boronda family of Rancho Los Laureles in today's Carmel Valley fell on hard times in the 1850s. Using a recipe that she claimed came from her father-in-law's home in Aragon, Spain, Doña Boronda made cheese to sell to neighbors for money to feed her 15 children. Jacks purchased her product and sold it as Jacks' Cheese.

Pebble Beach owner Samuel Morse wrote in a 1948 letter that "None of the Jacks family had anything to do with it." According to Morse, Domingo Pedrazzi, a Swiss-Italian dairyman in Carmel Valley, originated jack cheese in the 1890s. His process required applying pressure using a house jack. He called it Pedrazzi's jack cheese.

Whatever its origin, the semi-soft texture and mild flavor of Monterey Jack is America's preferred choice for grilled sandwiches and quesadillas.

EARTHBOUND FARM ORGANIC FOOD STAND

Where can I pick free organic herbs?

Drew and Myra Goodman started Earthbound Farms in 1984, long before organic farming went mainstream. To raise rent money and fund Myra's plans to attend grad school, they sold heritage raspberries from a roadside stand outside their 2.5-acre farm on Carmel Valley Road. As demand for organic products grew, they cooperated with other local farmers to sell their produce.

Three decades after opening the mom-and-pop farm stand, Earthbound Farms had grown to become the largest supplier of farm-fresh organic produce packaged as spring mix, baby spinach, and baby arugula to supermarkets and corner stores nationwide. In 2012, the Goodmans sold the company to a Colorado corporation for $600 million. One of the world's largest organic growers, Taylor Farms of Salinas, California, owns the business today.

ORGANIC ORIGINS

WHAT: Earthbound Farm organic food stand and cafe

WHERE: 7250 Carmel Valley Rd., Carmel, CA

COST: Free

PRO TIP: Myra Goodman has written several popular cookbooks, including *Food to Live By: The Earthbound Farm Organic Cookbook.*

Reaching over $50 billion in 2020, organic food sales in the US have grown about 300 percent since 2005. Fruit and vegetables comprise one-third of the total.

Earthbound Farms farm stand

After they outgrew their original location, the Goodmans repurposed buildings from Clint Eastwood's Mission Ranch into a larger, permanent stand. In 2003, they expanded the business and added an organic café. Taylor Farms continues to operate the property year-round, offering hot meals, sandwiches, coffee, ice cream, and an organic salad bar. Visitors are welcome to tour adjacent growing grounds with a resident expert organic gardener, and pick fresh herbs and berries from a kitchen garden at the rear of the stand. Some of the founders' original raspberry bushes have been transplanted here and continue to yield.

STARGAZING IN CARMEL AND BEYOND

Is Clint still mayor?

Monterey County has been a favorite movie location for the variety and accessibility of its scenery since Edison's cameraman shot *Surf at Monterey* in 1897. Pounding waves, brooding forests, rugged wilderness, and verdant valleys have starred in countless commercials, movies, and TV shows. The landscape has doubled for the coasts of New England, Old England, France, Norway, Russia, and elsewhere. Over 200 cinema and TV movies filmed here include *Basic Instinct*, *National Velvet*, *Play Misty for Me*, *Rebecca*, *Star Trek*, *Turner & Hooch*, and recently *Big Little Lies* and *Mad Men*. Locals turn out in droves for roles as extras, both for the cash and for the thrill of watching their favorite stars in action.

Many actors return to relax in their favorite settings. Gwen Stefani and Blake Shelton's whale-watching visit to Monterey in 2021 created a media frenzy. So did Elizabeth Taylor and Richard Burton in 1964, while filming *The Sandpiper* in Big Sur. Some of them decide to stay. The privacy of Pebble Beach and the cozy charm of Carmel appeal to show people. Doris Day and Clint Eastwood purchased hotels, the Cypress Inn and Mission Ranch, respectively, and lived in the area for more than 40 years. Both were familiar figures around town. Many visitors reported Eastwood sightings at the Mission Ranch piano bar.

Clint Eastwood served as mayor of Carmel from 1986 to 1988. He delivered on his campaign promise to legalize the eating of ice cream cones on the sidewalk.

Top: *Nicole Kidman and Reese Witherspoon on the set of* Big Little Lies *at Pacific Grove's Lovers Point*

Inset: *A Clint Eastwood campaign button for mayor of Carmel*

STAR SETTINGS

WHAT: Media stars work and play on the Monterey Peninsula

WHERE: Everywhere

COST: Free

PRO TIP: The Monterey County Film commission site (filmmonterey.org) lists all movies made in the area.

Visitors who stumble across a shoot say that it was the most enjoyable moment of their trip. If there are no productions underway, Doug Lumsen will be happy to take you on a narrated tour of the settings for past epics. His Monterey Movie Tours luxury theater on wheels shows video clips of locations that have starred in memorable movies.

AN EMPTY MANSION

What would you do with the property?

Gospel singers seeking "An Empty Mansion" don't have to wait to get to heaven. Carmel by-the-Sea has been trying to unload one for 50 years. What to do with a 6,000 square-foot "cottage" set in a bucolic nature preserve with a view of Point Lobos is a dilemma that continues to bedevil the city council. Designed by noted San Francisco architect Henry H. Gutterson in 1924 for Grace and Paul Flanders, the Flanders Mansion is a picturesque two-story, six-bedroom, four-and-a-half-bath, ivy-covered, Tudor Revival-style residence and carriage house.

Unable to develop the property as they wished after Mrs. Flanders passed away, the heirs sold the property to the city in 1972. Although two-thirds of city voters agreed that the mansion should be sold as a single-family residence, preservationists and neighbors thwarted the sale through years of litigation. Unable to dispose of the house, in 2019 the

FLANDERS MANSION

WHAT: A 1924 Tudor Revival mansion

WHERE: 25800 Hatton Rd., Carmel, CA

COST: Free

PRO TIP: No parking on-site; access is via trails through Mission Trail Nature Preserve.

As the Flanderses lost an earlier property to fire, they specified fireproof, precast interlocking concrete blocks as the primary building material—also a sound choice for earthquake country.

The Flanderses' Tudor-style residence is built with fire- and earthquake-proof concrete blocks.

council proposed a curatorship to allow a family to live rent-free for 15 years after completing specified repairs and upgrades. That plan is currently on hold.

Access to the property through Mission Trail Nature Preserve allows the public to examine the Arts and Crafts-era exterior details up-close. These include a steeply pitched gable roof in Gladding, McBean & Company's "Berkeley" russet ceramic tiles and heavy, Tudor-style arched doors and window shutters. A peek through the leaded glass windows reveals solid teak floors and carved interior walnut doors. It's fun to sit on a bench in the adjacent sunny meadow overlooking Carmel Bay and Mission and fantasize about what you could do with the property.

ANCIENT REDWOOD RESISTS FIRE AND DROUGHT

Where is Monterey County's oldest tree?

The blackened trunk of the Arthur Stone Dewing redwood tree is a testament to its centuries of resistance to drought, forest fire, and, more recently, the lumberman's axe. Tucked away in Williams Canyon off the Santa Lucia Preserve, this resilient redwood is estimated to be nearly 1,300 years old. Mature redwoods survive most fires because of their thick, insulating bark. As the oldest known coast redwood (*Sequoia sempervirens*) in Monterey County, the Dewing redwood has seen many fires over its lifetime, including recent major burns in 2016 and 2020.

The Dewing redwood, named for Harvard professor and author Arthur Stone Dewing (1880–1971), is on the Nature Loop trail of Mitteldorf Preserve of the Big Sur Land Trust (BSLT). The tree is 224 feet tall. Its crown of over 16,500 cubic meters is equivalent to the volume of 300 large school buses. Researchers have calculated that the tree has 500 million needles with a needle surface area that could cover 1.2 acres. Such large trees play an essential role in combating climate change by pulling carbon out of the air and locking it up in their bodies, a process called carbon sequestration.

THE DEWING REDWOOD

WHAT: Monterey County's oldest redwood tree

WHERE: Mitteldorf Preserve of Big Sur Land Trust

COST: Free to BSLT members

PRO TIP: Access to Mitteldorf is open to BSLT members and guests only.

The Dewing redwood dwarfs a hiker on the Nature Loop trail.

In addition to redwoods, Mitteldorf's more than 1,000 acres of riparian and oak woodlands, chaparral, and grasslands offer a variety of hiking opportunities and a lodge for youth education and wilderness experience programs.

Coast redwoods are taller than their inland cousins the giant redwoods (Sequoiadendron giganteum). But the latter are older, some more than 3,000 years old.

SAINT JUNIPERO SERRA, MIA

Where are they now?

Franciscan Father Junípero Serra led the Spanish missionaries who built a chain of missions across Alta (upper) California. He is one of the most revered and reviled figures in California history—revered by the faithful for establishing the Roman Catholic Church in the region but reviled for his role in the decimation of the indigenous peoples' way of life. Serra founded Mission San Carlos de Borromeo in Carmel, where he lived from 1770 until he died in 1784. Pope John Paul beatified him as the first saint on the North American continent in 1987. Pope Francis raised him to full sainthood during a visit to Carmel in 2015, an act that aroused applause and condemnation.

Angered by St. Junipero Serra's pursuit of mandatory conversion of native people to Christianity and abuse of the converts, a vandal toppled his statue on the mission grounds. Then someone decapitated his figure on a granite monument in Lower Presidio Park, Monterey. His severed head was found on the beach several months later and has been reunited with the body.

A life-sized redwood figure carved by Remo Scardigli for the Works Progress Administration (WPA) in 1937 is gone from Carmel's Devendorf Park. And the Serra Shrine, a roadside

Sculptor Joseph Jacinto "Jo" Mora's bronze and marble cenotaph of Serra reclining on his bier, surrounded by three missionaries, is safely housed in Carmel's Mission San Carlos.

Left: *The Remo Scardigli carving, formerly in Devendorf Park*

Right: *The empty Serra shrine*

niche at the entrance to the Carmel Woods subdivision that held an oak statue carved by Jo Mora in 1922, stands empty. Carmel city officials removed them in 2020 for safekeeping, following the widespread destruction of symbols of racism and colonialism across the country. According to *The Federalist*, since 2020, Serra was the third most popular target in the US to be defaced or removed, after Christopher Columbus and Robert E. Lee.

SERRA'S SARCOPHAGUS

WHAT: El Shrine de Padre Serra

WHERE: Serra Avenue and Guadalupe Street, Carmel-By-The-Sea, CA

COST: Free

PRO TIP: Late winter is the best time to avoid crowds at the mission.

PALO CORONA PARK, A SECRET NO LONGER

Why was this public open space largely inaccessible for years?

The Monterey Peninsula Regional Park District (MPRPD) acquired the 10,000-acre Palo Corona Ranch for use as a public park in 2004. Rising from near sea level to over 3,400 feet in elevation, the terrain ranges from riparian meadows along the Carmel River, to panoramic views of the ocean, and to steep, stream-carved inland canyons canopied by towering redwoods and pines. Because of limited roadside parking, entry required obtaining a permit in advance. So, as Palo Corona Regional Park, this wonderful public resource remained Monterey County's least-visited and best-kept open-space secret for more than a dozen years.

This changed in 2018 after MPRD acquired the adjacent Rancho Cañada Golf Club. The clubhouse is now a Discovery Center. The golf cart paths are walkways and the greens are being rewilded. Most important, parking is available for all who wish to visit the park. The trail map features three recommended hikes. The River Loop traverses a level floodplain under cottonwoods, willows, and ancient oaks. Rumsien Overlook is a one-mile hike over grassland, often in the company of grazing cattle, to a 250-foot elevation overlooking the river. Inspiration Point is a 1.5-mile steep walk up a graded dirt road to a bird's-eye view of the Carmel coastline.

PALO CORONA PARK

WHAT: Palo Corona Regional Park

WHERE: 4860 Carmel Valley Rd., Carmel, CA

COST: Free

PRO TIP: When hiking near cattle, approach slowly, speak in a normal voice and avoid walking between cows and calves. Move away quietly if they follow.

Palo Corona Park meadow trails seen from hikers' and bird's-eye perspectives

South of Inspiration Point, roughly 4,000 acres of rugged, unspoiled backcountry remain closed to public access. Trails could one day connect through the Ventana Wilderness to San Luis Obispo County. Backpackers, equestrians, and mountain bikers are eagerly awaiting decisions and funding to open this area for public use.

Wildlife in the park includes black bear, bobcat, deer, mountain lion, California condor, golden eagle, peregrine falcon, and spotted owl.

GREENE IN CARMEL

Why did it take nearly 100 years to get the right bell?

Brothers Charles Sumner and Henry Mather Greene's 1908 Gamble House in Pasadena, California, is considered one of the country's finest examples of Arts and Crafts residential architecture. Charles moved to Carmel in 1916, where he designed Seaward, a house perched on a bluff overlooking the ocean in Carmel Highlands for D. L. James. In a departure from his Craftsman style, locally quarried granite and sandstone walls and a Mediterranean tile roof appear to grow out of the cliff. The house is hidden behind a high wall at 105 California Highway One, but you can catch a glimpse through the trees from a turnout opposite the Hyatt Highlands hotel. Two other local works are less imposing but more accessible.

Greene built his own home and studio on Lincoln Street in Carmel-by-the-Sea on a more limited budget. In 1923, he acquired used bricks after a fire destroyed the El Carmelo Hotel in Pacific Grove. Working with his son, Greene selectively

GREENE ARCHITECTURE

WHAT: Home and studio of architect Charles Sumner Greene

WHERE: West side of Lincoln Street, three houses south of 13th Avenue

COST: Free

PRO TIP: There are no street numbers in Carmel-by-the-Sea. Properties are identified by a text description. See "Where" above.

Green Gables, a Greene-designed Arts and Crafts house and garden in Woodside, California, was listed for sale at $135 million in 2021.

Top left: *Greene's home on Lincoln Street*

Right and inset: *The memorial arch hung with the new bell on Ocean Avenue.*

removed layers of mortar to yield a bold, red-and-white, variegated bond pattern. A San Francisco lumber firm that supplied several major commissions donated oak and teak wood for doors, windows, and interior trim. Discarded redwood pickets from a ranch in Carmel Valley provided gate and fencing material for a multi-arched brick garden wall detailed with broken blue tiles.

His 1922 World War I Memorial Arch rises from the median strip of busy Ocean Avenue. It has presented an inviting target for wayward vehicles on several occasions. To mark the 100th anniversary of the city, members of the American Legion raised funds to restore and protect the sandstone pillars from damage and to replace the original bronze bell with one cast to the architect's specifications. Unable to afford Greene's original custom-designed bell, the builders had borrowed an existing bell from Carmel Mission.

THE STONEMASON POET

Why did he build a secret stairway?

A giant among American poets in the 1930s, Robinson Jeffers (1887–1962) moved to Carmel in 1914. Working with a local contractor and using boulders hauled from the beach over the next decade, he built a home for his family on a craggy promontory overlooking the bay. He named the tiny cottage modeled after a Tudor barn "Tor House." Tor is a word used in southwest England to describe a freestanding rock outcrop that rises abruptly from the surrounding landscape. Jeffers wrote all of his major works here. His poems, typically set in the rugged landscape of Big Sur, reveal a profound depth of learning inclusive of language, literature, myth, philosophy, and science. Charlie Chaplin, George Gershwin, Sinclair Lewis, and Charles Lindbergh were among many influential celebrity guests of the Jefferses.

Next to Tor House, Jeffers built Hawk Tower, named for a red-tailed hawk that visited while he worked, as a gift to his wife, Una. He used a block-and-tackle system to raise

TOWER OF LOVE

WHAT: Robinson Jeffers Tor House and Hawk Tower

WHERE: 26304 Ocean View Ave., Carmel, CA

COST: Guided adult tour fee is $12.

PRO TIP: Public access to Jeffers house and tower is by reservation. Check torhouse.org for details.

Jeffers's work enjoyed such wide national popularity that *Time* magazine featured him on the cover in 1932.

Hand-built structures by stonemason and poet Robinson Jeffers

rocks weighing up to 400 pounds up the 40 feet to the top of the tower. Between the rough granite boulders he embedded pieces of Big Sur jade, lava from Hawaii, and a stone he found on the beach near King Arthur's Tintagel Castle in Cornwall. He added a secret staircase for their twin boys. The tower became their favorite playground.

Most visitors prefer to climb the wide, external stairs to the top of Hawk Tower; the more adventurous tackle a narrow, secret passageway marked "Up Only." Dimly lit by one tiny window, the steep, corkscrew stairway requires careful maneuvering by its visitors to avoid getting stuck. Both routes lead to a lookout over crenellated battlements to the ocean.

JUNE GLOOM

Why is Carmel foggy and cold in summer?

The Monterey Bay area enjoys, or suffers depending on your point of view, the same cool, foggy summer weather that prompted someone to say, "The coldest winter I ever spent was a summer in San Francisco." (No, it wasn't Mark Twain. It has been traced back to an 18th-century English wit.) Beginning in June and extending to early fall, most coastal mornings start under a thick blanket of damp, gray fog. Sometimes it burns off in a few hours. It can also last for days. While it may dampen beach parties, the fog plays an essential role in moderating the coastal climate. The average summer high is 70 degrees Fahrenheit, and temperatures seldom reach the blistering levels that increasingly broil much of the country.

Why the summer fog? The earth's seasonal tilt on its axis causes ocean currents to move away from the shore. In a process called "upwelling," the displaced, warm surface water is replaced by cold water rotating up from below. As inland California warms in summer, it draws in air from the ocean. As it passes over the cold, upwelled water, damp air is cooled and its moisture condenses into droplets of fog. Sometimes you can stand on the beach as the "fog machine" turns on just a few hundred yards offshore and watch a billowing white cloud move steadily toward you. The warmer it gets inland, the foggier the coast.

The origin of the San Francisco weather quote is probably English actor James Quin (1693–1766). When asked if he remembered such a cold summer, Quin replied: "Oh, yes. Last winter."

June gloom forms over the ocean and rolls far inland.

As the fog creeps inland, it funnels into the Salinas Valley and the vineyards of the Santa Lucia Highlands. The resulting cool summer mornings encourage acid retention and concentration of aromatic compounds in wine grapes. A fine glass of premium Monterey County wine can go a long way to lift a severe bout of June gloom.

WINTER IN JUNE

WHAT: A thick blanket of damp, gray summer fog

WHERE: Everywhere along the coast

COST: Free

PRO TIP: Tank tops and short shorts are not recommended in summer. Bring a warm jacket.

THE DARK WATCHERS

"How does one find these creatures?"

For centuries, residents and visitors to the remote Ventana Wilderness area of Big Sur have reported sightings of tall, shadowy beings silhouetted on ridgetops. Others described eerie feelings of an elusive presence deep in the redwood-lined canyons. Early Spanish settlers called them *Los Vigilantes Oscuros* (The Dark Watchers). In his poem "Such Counsels You Gave to Me," Robinson Jeffers wrote that "They come from behind ridges to watch. He was not surprised when the figure turning toward him in the quiet twilight showed his own face. Then it melted and merged into the shadows beyond it."

John Steinbeck's mother, Olive Hamilton, told of leaving gifts of fruit or flowers for the watchers on her way to teach school in the area. He incorporated her tales of beings who roamed the hills into "Flight," one of his most widely anthologized short stories. Pepe Torres, a youth fleeing pursuers in the mountains, catches a glimpse of a mysterious

THEY FIND YOU

WHAT: The Dark Watchers

WHERE: Ventana Wilderness of the Los Padres National Forest

COST: Free

PRO TIP: Closed for several years after several devastating fires, Pine Ridge Trail, a rugged 20-mile hike through the heart of Dark Watcher country, reopened in 2021.

English and German writings of the 18th and 19th centuries describe the Brocken Spectre, a mysterious, magnified human shadow cast onto mist or cloud in mountainous areas.

Dark Watchers peer from ridges and hide in the deep forest.

black figure, "but he looked quickly away, for it was one of the dark watchers. No one knew who the watchers were, nor where they lived, but it was better to ignore them and never to show interest in them."

Explanations for the phenomena range from hallucinations induced by exhaustion or isolation to distant views of lone trees on ridgetops of the Santa Lucia Mountains. Steinbeck's son Thom preferred the mystical view. In his book *In Search of the Dark Watchers*, he posed the question, "How does one find these creatures? And the answer has always been the same; you don't find them, they find you."

THE SECRET VIOLENCE OF HENRY MILLER

If it's not a library, what is it?

The secret violence in the work of author Henry Miller "often lies dormant under a sort of languorous anticipation of the alert reader summoning its presence through reading." If, like this writer, you lack a sufficiently rigorous liberal arts education to fully appreciate the meaning of this quote by literary critic Katy Masuga, do not be discouraged. You can still enjoy a visit to the quirky Henry Miller Memorial Library near where he lived and worked from 1944 to 1962.

According to the website: "It is not a Library where you can borrow books, it is not a memorial with dusty relics, it is not a fully stocked bookstore, it is not a trinket store where you'll find t-shirts, mugs, and baseball caps or a selection of glossy photographs of the coast. It is not Henry Miller's old home . . . So, if it's none of those things, what is it?"

Founded a year after Miller's death in 1980 by his friend Emil White, the "Memorial Library" is a bookstore focused on the writer's work and legacy, but also much more. Located in a

---

NOT A LIBRARY

WHAT: Henry Miller Memorial Library

WHERE: 48603 Cabrillo Hwy. (Hwy. 1), Big Sur, CA

COST: Free

PRO TIP: Don't miss the whimsical sculptures alongside the entry path.

One of his easiest-to-read books, *Big Sur and the Oranges of Hieronymus Bosch*, is a Milleresque portrait of the place and the people he met while living there.

Top: Y2K, *a high-tech crucifix sculpture built from computer monitors by John Random.*

Inset: *Is this bust of Miller relegated to the bathroom intended as a critique of his work?*

grove of towering redwood trees, it is a gallery for local artists, an intimate concert setting for live performances, and an event space for the denizens of Big Sur. In short, it's a cultural experience for all. A red mailbox, boldly marked EMIL in yellow letters, still stands outside the gate.

Henry Miller is often confused with playwright Arthur Miller as the husband of Marilyn Monroe. The lyrics to Dan Bern's 1997 song "Marilyn," *Marilyn Monroe didn't marry Henry Miller, she lived outside the Tropic of Capricorn*, aim to put that straight.

THE GREATEST MEETING OF LAND AND WATER IN THE WORLD

Was Point Lobos the inspiration for Treasure Island?

One of the most frequently quoted descriptions of the rocky headland of Point Lobos State Natural Reserve—as "The greatest meeting of land and water in the world"—is widely, but erroneously, attributed to Robert Louis Stevenson, the author of the classic children's novel *Treasure Island*. Stevenson explored Point Lobos during his sojourn in the area in 1879 and, according to his daughter-in-law, "drew on Monterey scenery for his description of the island." However, no one has found the quotation or anything like it in his work or letters.

Glenna Collett, a top female golfer of the 1920s, wrote that artist Francis McComas was first to use the phrase to describe Point Lobos. Pebble Beach developer and owner Samuel F.

POINT OF THE WOLVES

WHAT: Point Lobos State Natural Reserve

WHERE: 62 Cabrillo Hwy. (Hwy. 1), Carmel, CA

COST: $10 per vehicle

PRO TIP: Arrive early—the popular reserve is frequently full and closed to vehicular entry after 9 a.m.

Point Lobos, named for a sea lion colony on the rocks of *Punta de los Lobos Marinos* (Point of the Sea Wolves) is today protected as a preserve referred to as "The Crown Jewel of the State Park System."

Big Dome on the flank of Whaler's Knoll at Point Lobos is possibly the inspiration for Stevenson's Spyglass Hill. And Stevenson was the inspiration for the Spyglass Hill golf course in Pebble Beach.

B. Morse also acknowledged McComas as the source but did not discourage other writers from using the same expression to promote his golf resort.

Morse, who had a passion for local history, suggested that RLS might also have roamed the hills and dunes of Pebble Beach across the bay from Point Lobos. He seized on that idea when choosing the name Spyglass Hill for a new world-class golf course in 1966. Starting with the first hole (called "Treasure Island"), 15 of the 18 holes are named after a significant place or character in the novel, as are many of the adjacent residential streets.

The founders of nearby Stevenson School reinforced the Pebble Beach-Stevenson connection by naming their institution, campus buildings, sports teams (the softball team are the Pirates), and newspaper after the author and passages from his novel.

GHOST TOWN ON PRIME OCEAN-VIEW REAL ESTATE

What makes it a "ghost town"?

Towering 300 feet above the Pacific Ocean's crashing surf, one of the West Coast's most faithfully restored ghost towns occupies prime ocean-view Big Sur real estate. Inhabited by chickens, a cow, and families with children until less than 50 years ago, the deserted barn, houses, and outbuildings of Point Sur Lighthouse cling to the edge of a great, volcanic rock with spectacular views of the coastline and the marble-topped peaks of the Ventana Wilderness.

The builders blasted 80 feet off the top of Point Sur in 1889, levelling the site to make room for a lighthouse along with homes, workshops, and gardens to serve the residents of a lightstation complex. Today preserved as Point Sur State Historic Park, it is described as a "ghost town" both for its collection of deserted buildings and for the shipwrecked souls and past keepers who

SHIPWRECK CENTRAL

WHAT: Point Sur State Historic Park

WHERE: Tours begin at a ranch gate on Highway 1, 19 miles south of Rio Road, Carmel, CA

COST: Adults $15, children 6-17, $5

PRO TIP: Tours at 10 a.m. Saturdays, 1 p.m. Wednesdays; no reservations, so arrive early

The solitary sentinel of Point Sur looks like an island but is connected to the mainland by a wide sandbar called a *tombolo*.

The lantern room of Point Sur Lighthouse atop the great volcanic outcrop

haunt the site. According to the Travel Channel, a tall man in dark blue, 19th-century garb lingers around the rock.

Although ghost hunters claim the lighthouse is one of the country's most haunted, tour guides offer no guarantees of a paranormal experience. They do promise a unique view into an 80-year time warp comprising the lighthouse, residences, and outbuildings, each restored to a key period of its service to the lightstation community.

THE NAVY
KEEPS ITS SECRETS

What are they not telling us?

Many secrets of the Cold War remain undisclosed at former US Naval Facility (NAVFAC) Point Sur. Under the guise of an oceanographic research station, the navy built a sonar listening post on this site in 1958. Cables with multiple hydrophones attached stretched for miles across the ocean floor. Technicians monitored undersea sounds for missile-carrying enemy submarines. Even inside the base, access to the cable terminal equipment building was severely restricted behind its own security fence and armed guard post. Nearly 40 years after decommissioning, the public still knows little about its activities.

The federal government donated the facility to California State Parks in 2000 but retained ownership of the cable terminal building. Barbed wire still secures this top-secret, windowless structure, and former personnel will not talk about their service. Naval scientists have confirmed that several hydrophones are still working. The readings are no longer analyzed to determine the presence of enemy submarines, and sonar signals generated by cruise ships, freighters, and whales go unheard.

The decommissioned facility is now incorporated into Point Sur State Historic Park. Central Coast Light Keepers,

---

Conspiracy theorists exchange stories of a secret Navy submarine base hidden in giant man-made caverns under Point Sur.

The top-secret cable terminal building remains off-limits to the public.

who lead docent tours of the adjacent lightstation, also offer walking tours of this sprawling campus of decaying, mid-20th-century buildings. Music from the theater, laughter from the officers' mess, and chatter in the communications center are long gone, replaced by hallways strewn with debris and the mournful whistle of wind through shattered windows.

KEEPS COLD WAR SECRETS

WHAT: US Naval Facility Point Sur

WHERE: 44350 Cabrillo Hwy. (California Hwy. 1), Big Sur, CA

COST: Adults $15, children 6–17, $5

PRO TIP: Tours offered on Saturdays and Sundays; no reservations, so arrive early

A GEOLOGY PROBLEM

Why is Big Sur prone to landslides?

Highway One through Big Sur is one of California's most popular scenic drives. More tourists traverse this narrow, winding road perched on cliffs high above the ocean than visit Yosemite every year—in years when traffic is not interrupted by floods and landslides, that is. Triggered by heavy rain in 2017, the Mud Creek slide closed the road for 14 months and deposited nearly 13 acres of new land onto the coastline below. Shorter closures are regular events. The California Department of Transportation (Caltrans) invests tens of millions of dollars into fixing the road annually. But a geology problem combined with winter storms that can drop more than a foot of water in 24 hours will ensure plenty more slides and road closures in the future.

The Santa Lucia Mountains are formed from ocean sediment churned by tectonic forces and thrust upward into one of the steepest coastal ranges in the contiguous United States. This loose rock mixture is extremely unstable, especially after fires remove vegetation cover, resulting in frequent landslides. Every day, rocks tumble onto the highway.

SLIPPERY SLOPES

WHAT: Pitkins Curve Bridge and Rain Rocks Rock Shed

WHERE: Half-mile west of Limekiln State Park

COST: Free

PRO TIP: Check that Highway 1 is open all the way to your destination before planning your trip.

Big Sur resident and blogger, Big Sur Kate, says: "The only questions we ever have is where it's going to close, when, and for how long."

East entrance to the Rain Rocks Rock Shed

For decades, Caltrans spent a million dollars a year to keep the road open at just one spot, appropriately called Rain Rocks. An innovative solution combined Pitkins Curve Bridge (landslide material flows under it) and Rain Rocks Rock Shed (boulders continue to fall, but over it). The California Department of Transportation also operates a continuous succession of rock plows, adapted from snowplows, to clear the road. Drive with extra care on the steepest stretches. Mother Nature can be arbitrary and capricious about when she rolls her rocks.

FREE AMMO

Why does a conservation organization distribute free ammunition?

With a wingspan up to 9.5 feet, weighing as much as 25 pounds, and able to fly up to up 150 miles in a day, the California condor (*Gymnogyps californianus*) is the nation's largest land bird. Due to loss of habitat, egg collecting, shooting, power line collisions, and poisoning, the population fell to just 22 birds worldwide by 1982. With private partners, such as the Monterey-based Ventana Wildlife Society (VWS), federal and state agencies worked with California zoos to establish a captive breeding program. They released the first captive-bred fledglings in 1992. Today, nearly 500 condors fly free across several western states and Mexico.

The number of wild births increases each year, but serious threats to the species' long-term survival remain. The most significant is poisoning from lead ammunition fired by hunters in squirrels, deer, and other unretrieved targets that become carrion for condors. Recognizing a problem with the cost and lack of general availability of copper ammo that is not toxic, VWS has a program of distributing free copper rounds to hunters within the condor breeding range. Sadly, although these efforts had been successful in steadily boosting the population over recent years, a dozen birds died due to pandemic-related disruption of the program during 2021.

All mature condors are tagged with a visible number. You can read the biography of each individual bird by looking up its number on condorspotter.com.

A condor over Big Sur

Photo courtesy of Tim Huntington

CONDOR RECOVERY

WHAT: Ventana Wildlife Society Discovery Center

WHERE: Near Andrew Molera State Park, 44550 Cabrillo Highway (California Highway 1), Big Sur, CA

COST: Free

PRO TIP: The center is open on Saturdays and Sundays, Memorial Day through Labor Day. Turn left on the dirt road before the state park entrance kiosk.

Learn about the condor project and other avian recovery activities at the VWS Discovery Center near Andrew Molera State Park in Big Sur. A "Bringing the Condors Home" exhibit includes information on the society's Big Sur wildlife sanctuary. Check ventanaws. org for condor cams in Big Sur and San Simeon that allow you to watch condors live with their chicks in season. VWS also works with other raptors, including bald eagles. Juvenile eagles released from the sanctuary between 1996 and 2000 led to a self-sustaining population today.

TEETERING ON THE PRECIPICE OF DEMISE

Is Deetjen's Big Sur Inn still open?

Helmuth Deetjen and Helen Haight moved to Big Sur in 1936 and purchased land by a creek in Castro Canyon. Helmuth hauled recycled materials from Monterey's Cannery Row to build a barn-like home and a collection of simple, Norwegian-style cabins. Decorated with furniture from Helen's antique business, they opened cabins to paying guests. Deetjen's Big Sur Inn became popular with travelers; some visitors stayed for weeks, while others were city folk seeking a few days' peace under the towering redwoods.

Helen died in 1962. When Helmuth passed away 10 years later, he offered his property to the state as a park and asked that it be maintained "in nearly the same manner and style" as during their lifetime. After the state declined the offer, his attorney created the nonprofit Deetjen's Big Sur Inn Preservation Foundation Inc. for charitable and educational purposes, with activities to include lodging to the public. As a unique slice of times past, it became a Big Sur institution and a destination that people revisit year after year.

"Teetering on the precipice of demise" is how managers have described the challenges of running the business along this remote and rugged coastline. Since the trust took over the property, there have been eight major forest fires, along

ICONIC INN

WHAT: Deetjen's Big Sur Inn

WHERE: 48865 Cabrillo Hwy. (California Hwy. 1), Big Sur, CA

COST: Rustic simplicity does not come cheap.

PRO TIP: There's no TV, no room telephones, and no cell phone coverage or Internet access on the property.

The rustic vernacular architecture of Deetjen's Inn

with floods, mudslides, and frequent road closures. The COVID pandemic, a fire, and extensive damage from falling trees led to "indefinite suspension" of operations. Deetjen's lovers worldwide rejoiced when the inn and restaurant reopened under new management in 2021. Buttermilk pancakes and funky, rustic amenities continue to resonate as a reminder of simpler times.

The inn was added to the National Register of Historic Places in 1990.

THE UPSIDE-DOWN RIVER THAT LOST ITS HEAD

What is an upside-down river?

At 175 miles from its headwaters in the Garcia Mountains south of Santa Margarita to the ocean at Monterey Bay, the Salinas River is Monterey County's longest. Millions of years ago, it was 60 miles or so longer. According to geologists, tectonic movement along the San Andreas Fault cut off flow from the original source in ancient Lake Corcoran that once filled California's Central Valley.

As water levels drop after the rainy season, the flow continues but is hidden from view deep beneath the visible riverbed. Locals call the Salinas the "Upside-Down River." In *East of Eden*, John Steinbeck described it as "only a part-time river" after the meandering course turns into a dry channel of rocks and sand in summer. Willows lining the banks continue to flourish throughout the dry season because their roots penetrate to the underground flow. This invisible reservoir serves as the primary

---

THE SALINAS RIVER

WHAT: Monterey County's longest river

WHERE: From San Luis Obispo County through the Salinas Valley to Monterey Bay

COST: Free

PRO TIP: Avoid the riverbank at the Salinas River National Wildlife Refuge during wildfowl hunting season, from mid-October to mid-January.

The Salinas is also unusual in that its flow is from south to north, instead of westward or southward like most other important rivers in the nation.

The two seasons of the Salinas River

source of irrigation water for Salinas Valley agriculture, the county's primary economic activity. More than 60 percent of the nation's lettuce and similar percentages of celery, broccoli, and spinach depend on this resource.

More recently, the Salinas suffered another reduction in length. Maps from the turn of the 20th century show the river running behind a dune-covered sand spit until reaching the ocean at Moss Landing. To drain the area for agriculture, farmers redirected the course in 1910 by breaching the spit at the present Salinas River National Wildlife Refuge site to allow water to drain directly into the bay. Wave-driven sand closes this outlet during the dry season, and water backs up into a lagoon that serves as a haven for wildlife.

A MOST EXTRAORDINARY MOUNTAIN

Where are the Vancouver Pinnacles?

When English explorer Captain George Vancouver took a horseback trip inland from Monterey in 1793, he came across "the sight of the most extraordinary mountain." In his book, *A Voyage of Discovery to the North Pacific Ocean and Round the World*, Vancouver described an imposing cliff face eroded into tall columns as like a "sumptuous edifice fallen into decay." A drawing by expedition artist and midshipman John Sykes is captioned "Remarkable Mountain near the River of Monterrey."

A 1903 *Sunset* magazine article claimed that Vancouver's "extraordinary mountain' was a peak in the Pinnacles. Images of "Vancouver Pinnacles" were presented in early efforts to establish the national park. In the 1950s, research correctly identified Sykes's drawing as Castle Rock, 50 miles away, off Highway 68 near Salinas.

REMARKABLE MOUNTAIN

WHAT: Castle Rock

WHERE: Inside the gated residential development of Markham Ranch

COST: Free

PRO TIP: Only residents of Markham Ranch have direct access to Castle Rock, but it can be viewed from Corral de Tierra Road.

Corral de Tierra, named after high, chapparal-covered ridges that enclose the valley, is variously translated as fence (or wall) of earth (or land).

The castle-tower-like eroded pillars of Castle Rock

Located near the entrance to the valley of Corral de Tierra, the eroded escarpment is known as Castle Rock for its resemblance to a fortified medieval castle. Towers and turrets reminiscent of Camelot fascinated a young John Steinbeck, who had been captivated by the tales of King Arthur and the Knights of the Round Table since he was nine years old.

Although the illusion of a great citadel evaporated when Steinbeck approached close to the ramparts, his fascination with the setting remained. Castle Rock forms the backdrop for several stories, including his novel, *The Pastures of Heaven*, which tells of the Monroe family, whose move into the bucolic valley precipitated trouble for the whole community.

THE BATTLE OF NATIVIDAD

Who won the battle?

In March 1846, US Army Captain John C. Fremont invaded Mexican territory by seizing Gabilan Peak, which at 3,169 feet is the highest point in the Gabilan Range east of the Salinas Valley. He raised the US flag and challenged Mexican forces to attack. Knowing that he was isolated without water on the top of a mountain, they ignored him. Fremont broke camp and departed after four days.

Angered by another incursion by Fremont's forces in November of that year, a group of Californios (Mexican citizens of Alta California) decided to relieve them of their horses. They clashed on Rancho Natividad near the foot of the peak. Four American soldiers died in the skirmish, but others escaped with their horses. The Californios reported no dead but five wounded. History records that they won the battle, but the interlopers won the war after the Treaty of Guadalupe Hidalgo (1848) ended the Mexican-American War and ceded California to the United States. California Historical Landmark #651, at San Juan Grade and Crazy Horse Canyon Road, Salinas, marks the site of The Battle of Natividad.

Fremont Peak (as the summit is now known) State Park features views across the Salinas Valley to Monterey Bay. Steep grassland slopes and pine and oak woodlands are home

Fremont Peak State Park is the site of an astronomical observatory with a 30-inch telescope, open for public programs on selected evenings.

Looking down from Fremont Peak toward the site of the battle.

to many birds and mammals. In *Travels with Charley*, John Steinbeck says the summit overlooked the "whole of my childhood and youth." He recalls exploring the lower slopes with his father seeking "cannon balls and rusted bayonets" remaining from the battle.

FIGHT SITE

WHAT: Fremont Peak State Park

WHERE: 11 miles south of San Juan Bautista at the end of San Juan Canyon Road

COST: Day use parking fee, $6 per car

PRO TIP: Fremont Peak straddles the border between Monterey and San Benito counties. Stand with one foot on either side of the summit and you'll be in two counties at once.

HAT IN THREE STAGES OF LANDING

What does it mean?

A monumental pop art sculpture by noted artists Claes Oldenburg and Coosje van Bruggen is an unexpected find in Salinas. Installed in Sherwood Park in 1982, *Hat in Three Stages of Landing* comprises three western-style hats skidding to the ground, as if tossed from the adjacent rodeo arena stands. Stylized with high crowns and downturned brims, the hats represent the diverse cultures of a community that favors this form of headwear for work and recreation.

Oldenburg explained how they came up with the hat idea: "In the climate of Salinas where so many work out-of-doors, hats are essential. Visiting a local hat store, we saw a wide range of headgear, from farmers' to ranchers' to ladies' garden hats. Coosje had already started a direction of thinking by noting down on

BIG HATS, NO CATTLE

WHAT: Monumental sculpture in a public open space

WHERE: Sherwood Park, 920 N Main St., Salinas, CA

COST: Free

PRO TIP: The park is named for Eugene Sherwood who donated the land for a public fairground.

Hats was the first of more than 40 large-scale collaborative projects executed by Oldenburg and van Bruggen across Asia, Europe, and the US.

Headwear, Western-size. California Rodeo Salinas stadium in the background.

her arrival: 'Something blowing in the wind . . . or something thrown . . . or something floating.' The subject of a hat fit well into this approach."

Fabricated of steel and aluminum painted with bright-yellow polyurethane enamel, each of the three hats are 18 feet long and 9.5 feet high. They are placed 80 feet apart, equidistant from one another, and each is set at a different height—the lowest almost touching the ground. In memory of van Bruggen and in recognition of their artistic partnership in creating the project, Oldenburg contributed to cost of the restoration and attended the rededication of the sculpture in 2013.

A MISSION, A HACIENDA, AND A HAUNTED FORT

Why did Julia Morgan build here?

Take a 25-mile detour off US Highway 101 south of King City, and you enter open, oak-studded San Antonio Valley. Hidden from the world outside by an arm of the Santa Lucia Mountains, the indigenous inhabitants called themselves *Te'po'ta'ahl*—"People of the Oaks."

At Mission San Antonio de Padua you can gaze on a landscape little-changed since the early 1800s, and the only California mission setting that its Franciscan founders might recognize. But turn and look in the other direction, and the paraphernalia of modern warfare assaults your senses.

Newspaper magnate and owner of Hearst Castle, W. R. Hearst, who purchased much of the valley land early last century, sold it to the US Government in 1940 for Army training as Fort Hunter Liggett. Acres of buildings, fighting vehicles, and an airstrip serve troop combat training activities, including field maneuvers and live-fire exercises.

The Hacienda, a Spanish Colonial Revival structure with a glistening, Moorish-style dome, stands in contrast to the surrounding drab, utilitarian military complex. Julia Morgan designed the building as a lodge to house Hearst's ranch workers and guests, including Errol Flynn, Clark Gable, Jean Harlow, and Will Rogers, in 1930. Today, the Hacienda serves as a hotel for army brass and families

Original (the Mission) and Revival (the Hacienda) Spanish Colonial architectural style buildings

visiting under the Army Morale, Welfare, and Recreation program. Although military personnel take priority for reservations, rooms at the Hacienda are also open to the public. You can stay overnight in one of the Cowboy Rooms, where the ranch hands bunked, or have a romantic getaway in the upstairs suite of Hearst's mistress, actress Marion Davies. Search under "Historic-Hacienda—Fort Hunter Liggett MWR" for hotel reservation information.

Pioneer Alice Halloran was decapitated in a wagon accident while fording the San Antonio River in 1898. Fort Hunter Liggett is said to be haunted by her headless ghost.

BE HERE WHEN IT HAPPENS

When will the next one hit?

Parkfield, a community of just 18 souls tucked away in southernmost rural Monterey County, sits astride the San Andreas Fault Zone. As one of the world's most closely scientifically observed earthquake zones, Parkfield promotes its notoriety as the "Earthquake Capitol of the World" [*sic*]. Historically, a 6.0-plus-magnitude earthquake has occurred every 22 years. The last one occurred in 2004—you do the math.

As you enter the town, a sign proclaims: "San Andreas Fault. Now Entering the North American Plate." Instruments buried near the fault constantly monitor temperature, pressure, magnetic changes, and other factors to help scientists understand the physics of earthquakes and faulting. These data are being used by the US Geological Survey to develop ShakeAlert, an early-warning system to deliver notice of an impending temblor to other areas of the state.

QUAKE CENTRAL

WHAT: The Earthquake Capital of the World

WHERE: Parkfield, CA

COST: Free

PRO TIP: If entering from Fresno County on the Parkfield-Coalinga Road, be aware that the surface is unpaved and impassable in wet weather.

If you want to stay longer, you can sign up for a cattle drive, or ropin', ridin', and relaxin' at a dude ranch weekend on the 20,000-acre V6 Ranch.

Black humor abounds at the Parkfield Café.

Seismic-related tourism centers on the Parkfield Café, where a slogan on the water tank urges, "Be here when it happens." The Parkfield Shakin' Burger is a popular menu item, and the proprietors advise, "If you feel a shake or a quake get under your table and eat your steak." Every Mother's Day weekend, this tiny community's population explodes to over a thousand bluegrass "pickers, pluckers, and fun-loving fans" for the Parkfield Bluegrass Festival.

STEEP AND NARROW

Who built those trails?

Named for its most distinctive feature, Pinnacles National Park is a massive granite outcrop of the Gabilan Range, eroded by wind and water into fantastic spires and twisted towers. Sited on the western side of the active San Andreas Fault, Pinnacles is the remnant of a volcanic flow near Lancaster in southern California 23 million years ago. Split in two by movement on the fault, the portion of the magma field that became the Pinnacles has travelled 195 miles northwest. According to geologists, if current rates of movement hold, Los Angeles will be adjacent to San Francisco in 20 million years.

Crews of the Works Project Administration built access roads and most of the 30 miles of hiking trails in the 1930s. One strenuous section of the High Peaks Trail, designated with some understatement as "Steep and Narrow" on the park map, has stairways with hand-chiseled footholds, sturdy guardrails lining cliff-edge switchback paths, and a tunnel through a towering granite monolith. It is not recommended for children or on hot summer afternoons, when temperatures often exceed 100 degrees Fahrenheit.

FAULTED TOWERS

WHAT: Pinnacles National Park

WHERE: 30 miles south of Hollister, CA or 10 miles east of Soledad, CA

COST: $30 per vehicle

PRO TIP: Arrive early; posted signs warn of possible one- to two-hour delays to enter. Take lots of water.

Maps show that Pinnacles can be reached from either east or west via Highway 146. Be aware that there is no connection through the park.

The Pinnacles' eroded volcanic spires protrude from the crest of the Gabilan Range.

Pinnacles supports some unique natural wildlife species. Talus caves formed by fallen rocks wedged between the walls of deep, narrow canyons provide habitat for colonies of rare bats. More than 400 bee species live here, one of the largest concentrations in the world. Pinnacles is also the only national park unit that manages a release site for captive-bred California condors. Early most mornings, you can watch them circling over the High Peaks area, searching for breakfast.

A SUITCASE CLONE?

Did he, or didn't he?

The Santa Lucia Highlands (SLH) is a small wine appellation on the west side of the Salinas Valley in Monterey County known for producing the West Coast's finest full-bodied and complex Pinot Noir vintages. The region's certification as an American Viticulture Appellation in 1991 was built on a viticulture heritage that began with European grapes introduced by Spanish missionaries in the late 1700s. Today, more than 50 vineyards span 22,000 acres on the east-facing mountain slopes of the Santa Lucia Range.

Convenient tasting rooms in Carmel make it easy for visitors to sample cool-climate Chardonnay and Pinot Noir SLH wines. If you prefer to visit the wineries, a half-dozen or so vineyards offer public tasting facilities along River and Foothill Roads in the Salinas Valley. This is still a laid-back experience without the glitz, crowds,

---

PINOT PERFECTION

WHAT: Santa Lucia Highlands vineyards

WHERE: River and Foothill Roads west of Gonzales, CA

COST: Charge for wine tasting

PRO TIP: Highway 68 is the most direct route from Carmel to the Salinas Valley. Carmel Valley Road is a scenic alternate through rugged country but is narrow, slow, and winding.

Santa Lucia Highlands grapes are blessed with a unique combination of abundant sunshine but cool climate, moderated by morning fog and brisk afternoon winds from Monterey Bay.

186

Santa Lucia Highlands vines thrive on a stony bench high above the Salinas Valley flatlands.

Photos courtesy of SLH-Vineyard Wine Artisans

and traffic of Napa Valley. You'll likely encounter more John Deere tractors than Porsches along this lesser-travelled wine trail.

A secret that has intrigued vineophiles over the years is the lineage of the pinot noir clone that makes Pisoni Vineyards "the Grand Cru site of the Santa Lucia Highlands" and Gary Pisoni its "rock star." Myth has it that, in 1982, the flamboyant vintner smuggled cuttings from Burgundy's legendary La Tâche Vineyard into California in his suitcase. Given the serious legal ramifications, Pisoni will not confirm the story, but does little to discourage its dissemination.

SOURCES

Where Zombie Worms Dine on Whale Bones: mbari.org; ocean.si.edu/ocean-life/invertebrates/zombie-worms-crave-bone; westernflyer.org

Rafts of Sea Otters: montereybayaquarium.org/animals/animals-a-to-z/sea-otter; elkhornslough.org/story; seaotters.com/sea-otter-viewing-tips

Turns Straw Into Gold: mrwmd.org/last-chance-mercantile; mrwmd.org/artist-in-residence

Purple Pipes Produce Productive Pastures: controlledrain.com/the-color-purple-what-does-it-mean-in-the-landscape-world; montereyonewater.org/216/Wastewater-Treatment; mercurynews.com/2020/01/27/new-water-recycling-projects-to-battle-seawater-invasion-in-monterey-bay-area

Where Marilyn Reigned as Artichoke Queen: phytophactor.fieldofscience.com/2008/02/artichoke-fruit-or-vegetable.html; seemonterey.com/food-wine/features/artichoke-tips; smithsonianchannel.asia/marilyn-monroe-as-california-artichoke-queen

Graffiti Portal to the Park: montereycountyweekly.com/news/cover/a-lot-of-monterey-county-art-exists-where-one-wouldn-t-normally-look-for-it/article_05efc9e6-ec42-11e3-9fe0-001a4bcf6878.html; parks.ca.gov/?page_id=580; digitalcommons.csumb.edu/fortord; sandcity.org/our-community/public-art; trailforks.com/route/comanche-s-grave; montereyherald.com/2011/03/02/fort-ord-trail-named-after-former-army-horse-soldier

Military Mementoes: trailforks.com/route/comanche-s-grave; montereyherald.com/2011/03/02/fort-ord-trail-named-after-former-army-horse-soldier

A Tale of Two Crosses: montereypeninsula.info/history/cross.html; montereyherald.com/2010/03/02/controversial-cross-to-stand-in-san-carlos-cemetery

World's Worst Car Show: 24hoursoflemons.com/concours-d-lemons; whatsupmonterey.com/events/monterey-car-week/concours-dlemons/444; wired.com/story/concours-d-lemons-car-show

Under the Flags of Four Colonial Powers: angelfire.com/dragon/volker/mty_historypath00.html; Celebrate Monterey's 250th Birthday with a virtual Tour; voicemap.me/tour/monterey-peninsula/monterey-state-historic-park-and-fisherman-s-wharf-walking-tour/sites

Weird, Wonderful, and Obscure Artists: montereyart.org; mhaadali.com

Feathered Pens and Hard Beds: cityofmonterey.oncell.com/en/010-colton-hall-birthplace-of-california-97638.html; monterey.org/museums/Monterey-History/Constitutional-Convention; monterey.org/museums/City-Museums/The-Old-Monterey-Jail

Legend of the Sherman Rose: cglhs.org/resources/Documents/Eden-3.3-Fa-2000.pdf; savingplaces.org/places/cooper-molera-adobe

Under the Influence of Satan: castateparks.oncell.com/en/409-robert-louis-stevenson-house-98497. html; rlsclubmonterey.org/newsletter-articles/rls-and-the-goat-ranchers; parks.ca.gov/pages/1080/ files/fa_455_003.pdf

And Now There Are Two: montereypeninsula.blogspot.com/2009/05/dennis-menace.html; latimes.com /archives/la-xpm-2001-mar-11-me-36206-story.html

Things That Go Bump in the Night: kazu.org/post/ghost-tour-takes-thrill-seekers-haunted-history-ride-through-monterey#stream; carmelmagazine.com/archive/14ho/reinstedt; toursmonterey.com/ gpages/ghomey.html

A Blueprint for Rock Festivals: montereypeninsula.blogspot.com/2008/11/monterey-pop-festival. html;

thisdayinmusic.com/liner-notes/the-monterey-pop-festival; history.com/this-day-in-history/the-monterey-pop-festival-reaches-its-climax

Monterey's Moon Tree: atlasobscura.com/places/monterey-s-moon-tree; slashgear.com/nasa-talks-about-where-moon-trees-ended-up-06658428; nssdc.gsfc.nasa.gov/planetary/lunar/moon_tree.html

Stairway to Huckleberry Heaven: alltrails.com/trail/us/california/huckleberry-hill-loop-trail; monterey.org/Portals/0/Maps/Huckleberry-Hill-Map.pdf; montereycountyweekly.com/people/ outside/stairway-to-heaven/article_b6d6a624-3ff3-11eb-ac1b-074b6637a7f7.html

Sloat's Sad Eagle: atlasobscura.com/places/sloat-monument; cityofmonterey.oncell.com/en/260-commodore-sloat-monument-97650.html

"The City Will Be Reduced to Cinders": nava.org/digital-library/raven/Raven_v15_2008_p107-118.pdf; davidlaws.medium.com/montereys-monumental-mosaic-mural-memorializes-marauding-mariners-more-3d6fa7f4881a; monterey.org/museums/City-Museums/Presidio-of-Monterey-Museum

Makk Rukkat: cityofmonterey.oncell.com/en/210-the-rumsien-people-and-the-rain-rock-97644.html; en.wikipedia.org/wiki/Rumsen; oyate.com/linda-yamane---ohlone.html

Blessing of the Fleet: noehill.com/monterey/poi_monterey_commercial_fishing.asp; voicemap.me/ tour/monterey-peninsula/monterey-state-historic-park-and-fisherman-s-wharf-walking-tour/sites/ fisherman-statue; italianheritagemonterey.org/stories.html; giamona.com/news.html

The Jazz Bus: metro-magazine.com/10032333/calif-s-mst-wraps-its-first-five-year-plan-with-the-monterey-jazz-festival; lighthousedistrict.net/news/2012/07/new-bus-rapid-transit-line-new-monterey-jazz; mst.org

The Queen of American Watering Places: library.nps.edu/hotel-del-monte; loc.gov/item/00694226; libguides.nps.edu/hoteldelmontetour/lanoviaroom

A Cornucopia of the World's Flora: denix.osd.mil/awards/upload/NSA-Monterey_CRM-IndT_ Narrative.pdf; pacifichorticulture.org/articles/rudolph-ulrichs-arizona-gardens; "Landscaping the Gilded Age," *Noticias del Puerto de Monterey* (Fall 2004).

Paths of History: parks.ca.gov/pages/575/files/MontereySHPFinalWeb080814.pdf; monterey.org/ Portals/3/PDFs/Links/exploremonterey_2011.pdf

"Mr. Gorbachev, Tear Down This Wall": *Babel-by-the-Bay*, Benjamin De La Silva (2015); en.the-wall-net.org/presidio-of-monterey-ca; montereyherald.com/2009/11/11/veterans-day-monterey-forgotten-vets-recalled-at-defense-language-institutes-wall-memorial

First Cathedral: atlasobscura.com/places/san-carlos-cathedral-2; montereypeninsula.blogspot.com/2008/11/graceful-carmel-mission-is-certainly.html; sancarloscathedral.org/wp-content/uploads/2012/10/Out-Lady-of-Gudalupe.pdf

Secret Gardens of Old Monterey: parks.ca.gov/?page_id=952; seemonterey.com/blog/post/10-secret-gardens-in-monterey-county; davidlaws.medium.com/historic-gardens-of-old-monterey-20efc79c579a

Secret Killers: montereybaywhalewatch.com/Features/feat0210.htm; pgmuseum.org/humpbackwhales; montereybayaquarium.org/animals/animals-a-to-z/humpback-whale

Secrets of the Ocean: guidebycell.com/clients/zoos-aquariums; montereybayaquarium.org/stories/how-pipes-work; montereybayaquarium.org/stories/exploring-a-chamber-of-nautilus-secrets; mercurynews.com/2011/09/01/new-great-white-shark-goes-on-display-at-monterey-bay-aquarium

Take the Chicken Walk: monterey.org/library/About-Us/Newsroom/bruce-ariss-was-here; davidlaws.medium.com/the-settings-for-the-stories-efdbc58455b2

Hollywood and Fish Hoppers: hmdb.org/m.asp?m=55162; canneryrow.com/our-story; canneryrow.org

The Ghost Railroad: abandonedrails.com/monterey-branch#; pacificgroveheritage.org/boardbatten/2004/01-2004-February-March.pdf; monterey.org/library/About-Us/Blogs/Monterey-Stories/the-del-monte-passenger-train

Great Parties at the Lab: monterey.org/museums/City-Museums/Pacific-Biological-Laboratories; atlasobscura.com/places/doc-ricketts-lab; atlasobscura.com/places/doc-ricketts-memorial

Ted's Dream: seemonterey.com/blog/post/new-statue-cannery-row-monument; innsofmonterey.com/blog/the-cannery-row-monument; mwg.aaa.com/via/places-visit/john-steinbeck-cannery-row-monument

Pacific Grove's Underwater Gardens: seaside.stanford.edu/hmlr; news.stanford.edu/news/2010/november/palumbi-monterey-bay-111210.html; seeker.com/the-woman-who-saved-monterey-bay-1765273860.html

John Denver Died Here: en.wikipedia.org/wiki/John_Denver; biography.com/musician/john-denver; roadsideamerica.com/tip/67930

Summer Places: en.wikipedia.org/wiki/A_Summer_Place_(film); pacificgroveheritage.org/newsletter/2008/HSNL_2008_01.pdf; nps.gov/nr/feature/places/pdfs/16000634.pdf; franklloydwrightsites.com/california/walker/walker_house.html

The Socialite Keeper: atlasobscura.com/places/point-pinos-lighthouse-2; columbian.com/news/2015/mar/29/point-pinos-lighthouse-continues-to-shine; pointpinoslighthouse.org; *Point Pinos Lighthouse Keeper Log*, Emily Fish (1893-1899)

Cool Critters of the California Current: trollart.com/category/murals; pgmuseum.org/online-exhibition; montereyherald.com/2015/04/13/murals-could-be-lost-after-pacific-grove-noaa-building-sale

The Great Tide Pool: *Beyond the Outer Shores: The Untold Odyssey of Ed Ricketts, the Pioneering Ecologist Who Inspired John Steinbeck and Joseph Campbell*, Eric Enno Tam (2005); *Cannery Row*, John Steinbeck (1945)

The Magic Carpet at Perkins Park: cityofpacificgrove.org/living/recreation/parks/perkins-park; kazu.org/post/pacific-grove-plans-revive-magic-carpet-its-former-glory#stream/0; davidlaws.medium.com/hayes-perkins-the-magic-carpet-man-1ca612b24c20; friendsofperkinspark.com

Hidden Treasures of the Museum: pgmuseum.org

"Much Baggage Is Not Desirable": visitasilomar.com/discover/asilomar-architecture; visitasilomar.com/discover/park-history

Where Otters and Whales Play in the Park: ksbw.com/article/whale-sculptures-create-controversy-at-berwick-park/8299977; montereyherald.com/2016/11/17/artist-behind-pacific-groves-whale-sculpture-wants-no-part-of-next-steps

J's Butterfly House: montereyherald.com/2015/03/16/pacific-grove-butterfly-house-a-labor-of-love/ pgmuseum.org/monarch-viewing; westernmonarchcount.org

He Could Have Been Bill Gates: computerhistory.org/blog/gary-kildall-40th-anniversary-of-the-birth-of-the-pc-operating-system; *They Made America*, Harold Evans, Back Bay Books (2004)

Flagpole Skater Breaks Record: youtube.com/watch?v=qjXhJ3yz0yY; 93950.com/steinbeck/ steinbeckdrive.pdf; *The Board & Batten* • Winter 2015/2016

Probing the Secrets of the Sea: stanfordmag.org/contents/bay-watch; hopkinsmarinestation.stanford.edu

Vagrant Hotspot: creagrus.home.montereybay.com/MTYsitesPtPinos.html; allaboutbirds.org/news/ birding-californias-central-coast; montereyaudubon.org/conservation

"For Entertainment, We Had the Library": pglibraryfriends.org; pacificgrovelibrary.org/about-library/ history-library

Where Sir Francis Drake Claimed Monterey for the Queen: *Pirates and Rogues of Monterey Bay*, Todd Cook (2019); *Treasures and Pirates*, Randall A. Reinstedt (1976)

Nowhere Else on Earth: ventanasierraclub.org/conservation/delmonte/pb_mont_pines.shtml; pebblebeach.com/insidepebblebeach/the-lone-cypress-stands-alone; roundtriptraveler.com/blog/ pebble-beach-17-mile-drive; pebblebeach.com/content/uploads/ResortMapWebsite-F11-13-18-FOR-OUTPUT-compressed.pdf; fs.fed.us/database/feis/plants/tree/hesmac/all.html; californiabigtrees. calpoly.edu/tree-detail/hesperocyparis-macrocarpa/41; macdirect.co.nz/know

The World's Most Famous Auto Beauty Contest: motor1.com/car-lists/most-expensive-new-cars-ever; pebblebeachconcours.net; pgrotary.org/annual-pacific-grove-concours-auto-rally

Play the Hay: pebblebeach.com/insidepebblebeach/introducing-the-hay-pebble-beach-the-tiger-woods-way; pebblebeach.com/golf/the-hay; pebblebeach.com/visitor-center

Bagpipe Tradition on the Links: pebblebeach.com/dining/the-lobby-lounge/bagpiper

Monterey Jack: Cheese Creation Myths: mchsmuseum.com/cheese.html; drinc.ucdavis.edu/dairy-foods/david-jacks-and-monterey-jack-cheese; sfchronicle.com/travel/article/The-competing-legends-of-Monterey-Jack-13655736.php

Earthbound Farm Organic Food Stand: earthboundfarm.com/about/our-farm-stand; earthboundfarm.com/about/our-heritage

Stargazing in Carmel and Beyond: montereymovietours.com; clinteastwood.net/mayor

An Empty Mansion: talesfromcarmel.com/2011/10/25/flanders-mansion; montereyherald.com/2019/04/12/determining-the-future-of-flanders-mansion; ci.carmel.ca.us/post/flanders-mansion-historic-photos

Ancient Redwood Resists Fire and Drought: montereycountyweekly.com/people/outside/monterey-countys-oldest-redwood-still-stands-after-soberanes-fire/article_489d46fe-5f60-11e6; bigsurlandtrust.org/mitteldorf-preserve-carmel-valley/the-arthur-stone-dewing-redwood

Saint Junipero Serra, MIA: montereyherald.com/2020/06/24/serra-statue-removed-in-carmel-for-safekeeping-local-cities-deciding-fate-of-others; montereycountyweekly.com/blogs/news_blog/carmel-removes-jo-moras-statue-of-father-junipero-serra-for-safekeeping/article_d53b9c1e-b5a6-11ea-b83c-e303b8bc3ea8.html; thefederalist.com/2020/07/22/list-of-183-monuments-ruined-since-protests-began-and-counting

Palo Corona Park, a Secret No Longer: mprpd.org/palo-corona-regional-park; mprpd.specialdistrict.org/files/f3e42f7ce/Item0617-12C_AmendDWSPCRPGDP_Attach4.pdf; seemonterey.com/blog/post/tales-from-the-trail-palo-corona-regional-park-carmel

Greene in Carmel: carmelbytheseaca.blogspot.com/2016/07/carmel-heritage-society-centennial-year_20.html; talesfromcarmel.com/2011/02/28/god-is-in-the-details-the-arts-and-crafts-home-of-charles-s-greene; gamblehouse.org/a-place-between-the-thunder-and-the-sun

The Stonemason Poet: torhouse.org/history; montereyherald.com/2009/04/01/the-mystique-of-tor-house

June Gloom: carmelrealtycompany.com/blog/how-much-fog-does-the-monterey-peninsula-really-get-420.htm; blog.pisonivineyards.com/notes/california-coast-fog-and-pinot-noir; anchorbrewing.com/blog/the-coldest-winter-i-ever-spent-was-a-summer-in-san-francisco-say-what-says-who

The Dark Watchers: sfgate.com/local/amp/dark-watchers-santa-lucia-range-stories-steinbeck-16012812.php; en.wikipedia.org/wiki/Dark_Watchers; darkwatchersbook.com

The Secret Violence of Henry Miller: *The Secret Violence of Henry Miller*, Katy Masuga, Camden House (2011); henrymiller.org; *Big Sur and the Oranges of Hieronymus Bosch*, Henry Miller (1957); henrymiller.org/2019/01/31/about-that-crucifix

The Greatest Meeting of Land and Water in the World: *Robert Louis Stevenson in California,* Katherine D. Osbourne (1911); pebblebeach.com/insidepebblebeach/the-nicknames-of-spyglass-hill-the-front-nine; parks.ca.gov/?page_id=571

Ghost Town on Prime Ocean-View Real Estate: pointsur.org; parks.ca.gov/?page_id=565; travelchannel.com/interests/haunted/articles/point-sur-lighthouse; medium.com/world-travelers-blog/point-sur-lightstation-a-haunted-ghost-town-on-ocean-view-big-sur-real-estate-cf3498132488

The Navy Keeps Its Secrets: medium.com/war-is-boring/the-navys-secret-undersea-lair-2d6b26e2b3b5; pointsur.org/documents/nav_fac.pdf; travelexaminer.net/point-sur-naval-facility-tour-reveals-cold-war-secrets

A Geology Problem: bigsurkate.blog/big-sur-interactive-highway-maps-with-slide-names-mile-markers; mercurynews.com/2014/01/16/big-sur-rock-shed-a-dramatic-covering-for-highway-1; discover-central-california.com/rain-rocks-rock-shed.html

Free Ammo: medium.com/creatures/close-encounters-of-the-condor-kind-77077878cd25; ventanaws.org

Teetering on the Precipice of Demise: deetjens.com; en.wikipedia.org/wiki/Deetjen%27s_Big_Sur_Inn

The Upside-Down River That Lost Its Head: soulofca.org/the-upside-down-river; *The Salinas: The Upside Down River,* Anne B. Fisher (1945); seymourcenter.ucsc.edu/OOB/100_Meandering%20 River%20Mouths.pdf

A Most Extraordinary Mountain: *A Voyage of Discovery to the North Pacific Ocean and Round the World Vol. IV,* Captain George Vancouver. (pg. 1423); corraldetierra.com/history.html

The Battle of Natividad: ohp.parks.ca.gov/ListedResources/Detail/651; worldhistoryproject. org/1846/11/16/battle-of-natividad

Hat in Three Stages of Landing: oldenburgvanbruggen.com/largescaleprojects/hats.htm; weirdca.com/location.php?address_id=31; salinas411.org/hat-in-three-stages-of-landing

A Mission, a Hacienda, and a Haunted Fort: missionsanantonio.net; hunterliggett.armymwr.com/programs/historic-hacienda

Be Here When It Happens: seemonterey.com/regions/parkfield; v6ranch.com; shakealert.org

Steep and Narrow: nps.gov/pinn/index.htm; nps.gov/pinn/learn/nature/bees.htm; geolsoc.org.uk/Plate-Tectonics/Chap3-Plate-Margins/Conservative/San-Andreas-Fault

A Suitcase Clone?: santaluciahighlands.com; pisonivineyards.com; nytimes.com/2008/10/22/dining/22pour.html

INDEX